GARDEN TOURS
OF
ENGLAND

Self Guided Tours
of the
COTSWOLDS

Bonnie Randall

**Photographs and Illustrations by
Greg Randall**

Windsor Hill Publishing

Illustrations, Maps & Photographs: Greg Randall
Cover Design: Greg Randall & Bonnie Randall

Distributed U.S.A.: Windsor Hill Publishing

Library of Congress Catalog Card Number 96-091014

Randall, Bonnie, 1949-
Garden Tours of England- The Cotswolds
1. Garden Tour- England, 2. Guidebooks, 3. Cotswolds

ISBN-0-9656510-0-2

Printed in the USA by

*M*ORRIS
PUBLISHING

3212 E. Hwy 30
Kearney, NE 68847
800-650-7888

Cover Photo: Brook Cottage, Oxfordshire, England

To my husband for having faith in me and
for encouraging me to try something
completely different.

Dovecote at Rousham Park, Oxfordshire

• TABLE OF CONTENTS •

Charming thatched roofs of Cotswolds cottages.

• INTRODUCTION •

My husband and I started visiting the wonderful gardens in England several years ago. In preparation for each trip we assembled our collection of picture books, guide books, garden books and the atlas and proceeded to map out our trip. We spent what seemed like days and, although it was a labor of love, it was a very complicated process.

The goal of this book is to take most of the confusion and complications out of your planning. It will provide you with the information and directions you will need to really enjoy your trip. Remember, unlike in the U.S., every garden is not open daily from 9:00 to 5:00. In fact, some gardens are only open one day a week and some are only open between 2:00 and 6:00 in the afternoon. Directional signs are, let's face it, different and not always terribly clear. Then there are those roundabouts and you have to drive on the left hand side of the road. Well, believe me it's all worth it and this book will make your trip a lot easier.

I selected the Cotswolds for this first book because it is one of my favorites. It is a beautiful region of England with quaint little villages tucked into some of the most glorious and fertile valleys in the world. There are thatch-roofed homes, Cotswold stone walls, and lovely pastureland not to mention some of the most wonderful gardens in Europe. Its a small territory, covering about 55 miles in length and 75 miles in width so you will be able to stay in one or two locations and see it all!

This book describes 21 tours. They are organized by day of the week, with the intention that you will not have to drive far between gardens or feel the need to rush from one to the other. First, determine the day (or days) of the week that you have available. Then find the tours that are open on those days and finally, select the specific tour (s) you are interested in. Brief descriptions and histories of each garden are provided to help you make your selection. Under "List of Publications" you will find several suggestions for colorful picture books that focus on this region and there are many more to choose from in your local book stores. Purchase one or two and get a glimpse of the wondrous gardens that await you.

There are many kinds of gardens in these tours. Some are beautiful flower gardens with herbaceous borders and climbing roses. Some are very formal with large fountains and glorious sculptures and for some, the beauty is found in the history and architecture. For all of the gardens, the enjoyment is in the whole, the design, the history, the house (castle or manor), the countryside and the garden. Take time to experience it all!

There's a lot to see and no time to waste, so lets get started!

GARDEN TOURS
OF
ENGLAND

THE
COTSWOLDS

ENGLAND
MAP

COTSWOLDS
MAP

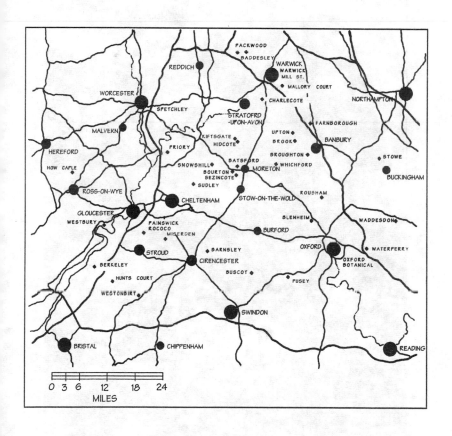

Climbing roses adorn this Cotswold stone wall.

• THE COTSWOLDS •

The word Cotswolds comes from the Saxon phrase "hills of sheep coats" (cot is the biblical term for enclosing sheep, wold means rolling hillside). Although tourism has now become a major part of the Cotswolds' economic strength, for hundreds of years the wool industry played an important role in the economy of this region.

By the 14th century so many acres of woodland had been cleared for farming that the land had reached its maximum use. Looking for better sources of livelihood, farmers turned more and more to sheep; pastureland increased and the wool trade flourished. In the 20 years following the Domesday census, the sheep population outnumbered people by 4-1. At the height of its prosperity, tax revenue from the wool trade accounted for over one half of the total wealth of England and Cotswold wool was famous throughout Western Europe.

The decline of the woolen industry occurred in the first half of the 18th century when crippling taxes forced merchants into bankruptcy. Cloth making took over as a major industry in the region until the Industrial Revolution introduced more economic ways of producing cloth. Cloth making was centered in Stroud where there was water power to run the mills.

The Cotswolds sit on an elevated land mass made almost entirely of oolitic limestone. This great limestone belt begins at the Dorset coast and sweeps northwest till it ends at the Humber. The Cotswolds' hills cover the major portion of Gloucestershire, all north Oxfordshire, a tiny piece of Warwickshire and several bits scattered about Worcestershire.

Everyone talks about "Cotswold stone" but it is just basic limestone. The secret is that this limestone is easily worked which allowed it to be used on the most humble buildings, such as barns and pigsties, as well as the grand manors and churches of the region. This uniformity of construction material adds to the charm and beauty of the area.

You will find various colors of stone. This is created by the different percentages of mineral iron in the limestone. The north quarries have a honey colored stone. Burnished gold stone comes from the Guilting Stone quarry at Goscombe. The central quarries have pearly white stone and the south produces soft gray.

Few of the quarries are still in operation but you can see abandoned workings all over the countryside.

The rivers all run north to south and join the Thames on the east side of the Cotswolds and the Severn on the west side. These rivers are more than just part of the lovely scenery but are also functional in providing a dependable water supply. Without this water to provide power for the mills, few of the "wool" churches that stand out on the skyline, the great country houses or the gardens you are here to visit, would have been built. Many of the grand churches found in this region were built by wool merchants, therefore the name "wool" churches.

Most of the towns and villages are not built along the tops of the hills but comfortably tucked away in the valleys. When driving along the hill top roads across the Cotswolds, you can look down into these cozy and picturesque little spots.

Hardly any Cotswold towns were planned, they just happened. Most villages can claim Saxon roots, their names have Anglo-Saxon origins and they were included in the Domesday census. Buildings, distinctive in style, are constructed of the indigenous limestone and roofed with either local slate or thatch.

As you drive through the countryside, you will find the fields separated by a criss-cross of wonderful "dryset" Cotswold stone walls. These stacked stone walls appeared between 1700 and 1840 when 120,000 acres of open land were enclosed by Acts of Parliament.

A few of the towns and villages you may encounter in your travels are:

Chipping Camden (chipping means market), one of the Cotswolds great treasures, is an ancient "wool" town. It has remained little changed and unspoiled for the last three hundred years. During your visit you will find a glorious 15th century church, an early 17th century market hall, several thatched roofed cottages, colorful gardens and inviting inns and restaurants. C.R. Ashbee brought the Guild of Handicraft to Chipping Camden in 1902. Its members had a considerable influence on the area in the early 20th century. The Ernest Wilson Memorial Garden in Chipping Camden was dedicated to "Chinese" Wilson, a collector of rare plants from China. Many plants bear his name in their Latin botanical name, i.e. Ilex wilsonii.

Bourton-on-the-Water is referred to as the "Venice of the Cotswolds" because the River Windrush flows lazily through the middle of town. As you stand on one of the camel-backed bridges that span the clear waters you can look down and see fat trout swimming by. The first bridge over the Windrush dates back to Roman times.

The truly quaint Upper and Lower Slaughter are numbered among the "water villages" of the Cotswolds. We have enjoyed several visits here and it would be a good place for a peaceful stop during your hectic day of touring.

Stow-on-the-Wold, at 800 feet, is the highest town in the Cotswolds. It was recorded that as many as 20,000 sheep were sold on one occasion at one of the great sheep fairs in this hill town.

Circencester, second only to London under the Romans, also flourished with the wool merchants. If you visit here you will find its medieval character surprisingly preserved. Circencester Park has a yew hedge so high that you might find someone standing on a fireman's ladder to do the clipping.

Stanton, surrounded by some of the lushest greenery in England, contains some of the best mid-16th to mid-17th century Cotswold architecture and some of the lovliest village gardens.

In Broadway the houses and cottages face each other across the historic road that runs from London to Worcester. William Morris, an influential designer and writer of the 19th century, visited often and encouraged his artist friends to spend time here. Even Charles I and Cromwell stayed here (although I doubt at the same time) and the accommodations and shopping are still superb. There is even a Teddy Bear Museum (most important to me) with 400 bears and the earliest known Steiff bear c. 1903.

Stratford-upon-Avon, once a medieval market town and the home to William Shakespeare, is now quite the tourist attraction.

Oxford is the home of one of the great places of higher learning in the world. It is made up of a number of colleges including Merton College founded in 1264. The Merton Library, the first Renaissance library in England, was built in the 1370's. You will find many places to explore but watch out for professors flying by on their bikes with their black gowns billowing out behind them.

• HELPFUL HINTS •

• The maps you will find in this book are good. They are drawn to scale and you should have no trouble following them but, an atlas or road map of England is a must! There are numerous country roads and if you take a wrong turn, you can get confused and lost very quickly. Maps are available at book and travel stores and you should pick one up before you leave.

• Wear comfortable shoes. You will be doing a lot of walking and most of the time it's on dirt or gravel and up and down stairs.

• Wear comfortable clothes. In the summer you may be able to dress light but always bring along a sweater or sweatshirt and possibly a lightweight jacket. Warmer clothes will probably be needed in the spring and fall. A rain coat or slicker is good too.

• Make sure an umbrella is available all year round. We've been very lucky in all our trips but that doesn't mean you will be.

• Bring lots of film. Although there is film and disposable cameras everywhere, it's never around when you really want it and it's usually more expensive.

• Keep your eyes and ears open, many private homes open-up their gardens to the public one or two afternoons a year. If you are lucky, you might have the opportunity to visit a few. Look for signs along the road or in the towns and villages you are visiting. Also, *The Yellow Book* on the "List of Publications" can be ordered and will provide a lot more information on local gardens.

• This area is chock full of charming inns and B&B's; The Malt House in Broad Campton, Kings Arms in Chipping Camden, Old Parsonage in Oxford, the Swan Hotel in Bibury, the Hinton House in Ablington are but a very few. See "List of Publications" for further information or contact your travel agent.

• Many of the gardens have food services for lunch and/or tea. Usually nothing extravagant but frequently tasty (some of the pastries at tea are great). There is also hearty fare at most of the pubs and there are little restaurants in many towns and villages.

Hints (continued):

• I recommend you join the National Trust if you plan on visiting three or more National Trust gardens during your visit (two people, six total admissions). Your yearly membership allows free admission to all N.T. properties, a discount on some merchandise and a year of N.T. publications. See the following page for more information on the National Trust.

• The guide books and maps you find at many of the gardens are invaluable and are usually worth the few pounds. The National Trust books are especially good.

• Transportation: There are several types of transportation available. The simplest is to rent a car and drive yourself. You will be driving on the left side on very narrow roads but it won't take long to adjust. Mid sized cars are the best and ask for an automatic unless you are experienced with a stick. Autos can be rented at the airports and in many of the larger cities. Check with your travel agent or your favorite rental company for locations and availability before you leave on your trip. Remember, our maps are good but you really do need an atlas or a good road map of England.

You can also rent a car with driver. This is a relaxing way to travel especially if you just want to take a couple day trips. Although, in many cases, the cars are sedans not limos, they are very comfortable and you can just sit back and enjoy the countryside. If you are as lucky as we were on a couple of occasions, your driver will be a retired major or history professor with some wonderful stories about the towns and taverns you see. You can let your finger do the walking or you can ask at your hotel. This is a common practice and should be readily available even in some of the smaller towns.

Trains can be fun. If you are staying in London and want to spend a few days in the country, you can take a train to a central location such as Oxford or Stratford-upon-Avon and rent a car or a car and driver there. The trains in Britain are great! They are clean, safe and on schedule. First class is worth the few extra pounds. Information on passes and schedules are available through your travel agent or the British Tourist Board.

- Many of the gardens in this book are open on days other than those listed in the tours. See Garden Particulars on pages 132 & 133 for further information.
- The months, days and times of operation were confirmed prior to publication of this book. Keep in mind that changes may be made to these schedules. It is advisable to confirm the times prior to setting out on your day's tour.

THE NATIONAL TRUST

The National Trust, a registered charity, was set up in 1895 to promote "the permanent preservation, for the benefit of the nation, of lands and tenements (including buildings) of beauty or historic interest". The Trust currently cares for almost 600,000 acres of outstanding countryside, 555 miles of unspoiled coastline and has more than 300 historic houses and gardens open to the public.

The Trust is able to declare its property "inalienable" by an Act of Parliament in 1907. This means that once land and buildings are in the Trust's ownership, they can never be sold or mortgaged (although they can be leased). Ownership by the Trust guarantees protection for generations to come.

Memberships in the National Trust provides 45% of the annual income needed by the Trust to look after its properties. Members are given free admission to houses and gardens in its care in recognition of the support members give the Trust.

Americans can also join The Royal Oak Foundation which is the U.S. membership affiliate of the National Trust. The Royal Oak foundation actively supports the Trust's missions and promotes cultural exchanges through scholarships and internships.

Ask about becoming a member at any National Trust garden or contact the Royal Oak Foundation at 285 West Broadway, Suite 400, New York, N.Y. 10013-2299, (212) 966-6565, fax (212) 966-6619.

Kiftsgate Court, Gloucestershire

TOURS
OF THE
COTSWLDS

TOUR #1
MAP

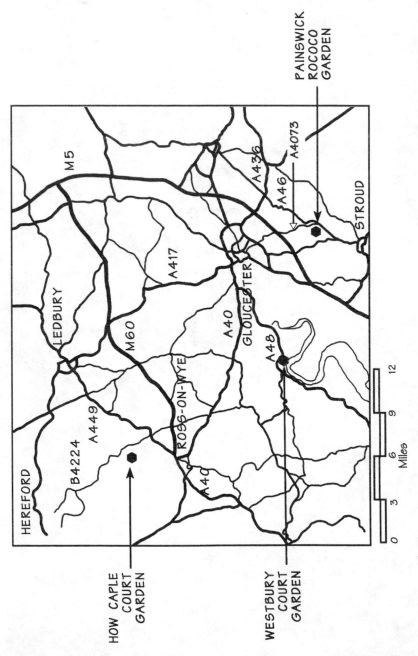

TOUR #1

* PAINSWICK ROCOCO GARDEN
* WESTBURY COURT GARDEN
* HOW CAPLE COURT

• WEDNESDAY THROUGH SATURDAY •

A historic group of gardens that provides wonderful examples of different architectural designs and styles. Time needed for your visit to each garden is a minimum of one hour. Travel time between Painswick Rococo and Westbury Court is 30 minutes. Travel time between Westbury Court and How Caple is 45 minutes.

PAINSWICK ROCOCO GARDEN

- Hours of Admission: 11:00 to 5:00
- Location: half mile outside village of Painswick on B4073

- This garden is historically significant since it is the only complete survivor from the 18th century Rococo period.
- Rococo in garden design means a compromise between formality and informality, it is characterized by elaborate and profuse ornamentation and, in this case, is done with delicacy and refinement.
- The manor was built by Charles Hyett in 1735, his son Benjamin created the garden in the 1740's
- The restoration of this 6 acre garden began in 1984 and was aided by a Thomas Robins painting dated 1748.
- You will find several interesting buildings and structures including the Red House, a Rococo style garden house.
- The Excedra Garden is a lovely perennial garden planted with 18th century type plants. There are over 20,000 plants and bulbs and colorful from early spring through late fall. The last time I was there it was bright and cheerful with irises, foxgloves, columbines and many more.
- Look for the large kitchen garden. It is surrounded by a wooden fence with espaliered trees. A cute little scarecrow protects the garden and the birds just love him.

Rococo structure found in the Excedra Garden.

WESTBURY COURT GARDEN (N.T.)

- Hours of Admission: 11:00 to 6:00
- Location: 9 miles southwest of Gloucester on A48

  - This garden is one of the rarest types of gardens to survive in Britain, a formal late 17th century water garden that was influenced by Dutch ideas.
  - It was laid out by Maynard Colchester. Digging of the Long Canal began in 1696. The T-Canal and Gazebo were probably built around 1715 by Colchester's nephew, Maynard Colchester II.
  - A manor house no longer exists, the original house was demolished in 1805 and the Victorian house was demolished in 1960.
  - The old Dutch style has been closely adhered to during the recent restoration and replanting. (1967 National Trust)
  - The Tall Pavilion or summerhouse was originally built in 1702-3 by Colchester and rebuilt by the Trust. If you climb to the top you will find a small display of the history and a view of the entire layout of the garden.
  - A wonderful Neptune fountain stands at one end of the T-Canal and the two canals are bordered by yew hedges topped by topiaries.
  - In the small Walled Garden you will find almost 100 species of plant types grown in England before 1700 plus 40 kinds of old roses from same period. The effect of the soft colors on this small garden is quite nice.
  - The espaliered fruit trees along the walls are old varieties carefully researched & propagated.
  - Standing straight and tall not far from the pavilion is a magnificent 400 year old Holly Oak, one of England's great trees.

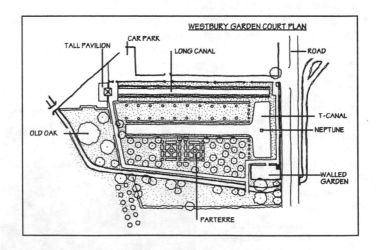

WESTBURY GARDEN COURT PLAN

Florentine water garden at How Caple Court.

HOW CAPLE COURT

- Hours of Admission: 10:00 to 5:00
- Location: 10 miles south of Hereford on B4224; turn right at How Caple crossroads

  - An interesting 11 acre Edwardian garden set high above River Wye with views of the Forest of Dean and the Welsh mountains.
  - A large, rolling expanse of lawn with a variety of mature trees provides a peaceful respite in a busy day of touring.
  - Cotswold stone walls surround three levels of formal terraces planted with many varieties of richly colored perennials.
  - You will find a rose garden with yew hedges, shrub roses and more mature trees.
  - Look for the wonderful specimen Japanese maples. Not as common in English gardens as you might expect, these are some of the largest I've ever seen.
  - The sunken Florentine water garden is under restoration.
  - There is also a newly restored Mediaeval Church.
  - Note: a small nursery outside gate sells roses and perennials (fun to look around).

OTHER GARDENS IN THE AREA: BERKELEY CASTLE, HUNTS COURT, MISERDEN PARK

TOUR #2
MAP

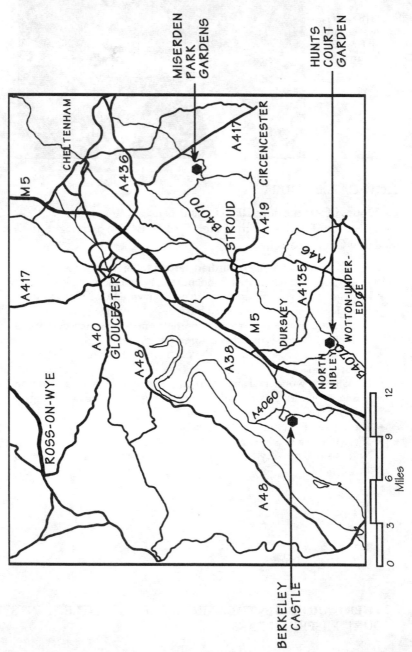

■■■■■■■ ■■■■■■■■■■■■■■■■■■■■■■■■■■■■■■■■ ■■■■

TOUR #2

* HUNTS COURT GARDEN
* MISARDEN PARK GARDENS
* BERKELEY CASTLE

• TUESDAY, WEDNESDAY, THURSDAY •

If you love roses as much as I do, you will need at least two hours at Hunts Court. Some of the loveliest borders can be found at Misarden and if Robin Hood has always been one of your favorites, Berkeley Castle is the place for you. Time needed for your visit to Misarden and Berkeley Castle is a minimum of one hour each. Travel time between Misarden and Hunts Court is 40 minutes. Travel time between Hunts Court and Berkeley Castle is 20 minutes.

HUNTS COURT GARDEN

- Hours of Admission: 9:00 to 5:00
- Location: 2 miles northwest of Wotton-under-Edge; from Wotton B4060 Dursley Rd turn right in Nibley at Black Horse Tavern

  - A 20th Century garden, this 2.5 acres with great views was created over the last 20 years by Keith & Margaret Marshall
  - You will find a remarkable collection of 400 varieties of roses including species, albas, damasks, gallicas and bourbons.
  - Numerous trees and shrubs have been planted to complement the roses and the paths meander to give you a quiet, peaceful feeling.
  - The Sundial Garden contains a large collection of penstemons along with many other herbaceous perennials
  - Look for each of the 30 varieties of hardy geraniums and the outstanding collection of 60 shrubby potentillas.
  - There is beauty in all seasons here including the autumn color of the trees.
  - Note: A wonderful nursery to visit even if you can't take anything home. There is a huge selection of roses, most are never seen in the States.

■■■

Manor House and Wisteria covered Peristyle at Misarden.

MISARDEN PARK GARDENS

- Hours of Admission: 9:30 to 4:30
- Location: 6 miles northwest of Circencester follow the signs off the A417 or from Stroud take B4070

  - This beautiful house stands high overlooking Golden Valley and provides great, panoramic views.
  - A wonderful example of the use of land on a hillside. The house sits on a broad cut terrace and the terracing and sloping away of different gardens creates spectacular spaces and marvelous vistas.
  - The original house was built in 1620 by Sir William Sandys but it has been somewhat altered by several owners since the early 19th century.
  - The walled garden is one of the prettiest I've ever seen. You will find a double border of herbaceous plants facing two additional borders and creating a riot of color.
  - A narrow grass path is edged by yew hedges clipped into domes on top, well done.
  - The formal rose garden has been newly replanted.
  - You will also see a lovely gate house and a quaint old church.

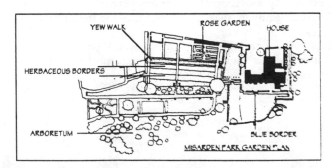

BERKELEY CASTLE

- Hours of Admission: 2:00 to 5:00
- Location: at Town of Berkeley on B4066

- This formidable castle has been home to the Berkeley family since the 12th century.
- You will see a garden of simple terraces with grass walks and narrow, low growing borders. Not the color you may see in other gardens but beautiful in its own right.
- Four levels of terraces are planted with a wide selection of drought tolerant, sun-loving and tender plants.
- Enjoy the terrific assortment of climbing wall plants including evergreen magnolias, banksian roses, clematis and a wisteria that rises the whole height of the castle.
- There is also a lovely formal lily pond.
- Note: A "Robin Hood" castle in excellent condition, it conveys a wonderful touch of medieval romance.

Berkeley Castle overlooking the wonderful formal Lily Pond.

OTHER GARDENS IN THE AREA: BARNSLEY HOUSE, PAINSWICK ROCOCO GARDEN, WESTBURY COURT GARDEN, WESTONBIRT ARBORETUM

TOUR #3
MAP

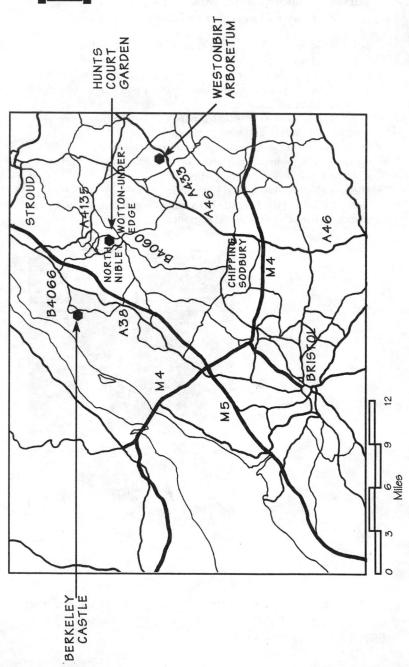

HUNTS COURT GARDEN

WESTONBIRT ARBORETUM

STROUD

A4135

NORTH NIBLEY

WOTTON-UNDER-EDGE

B4060

A433

A46

A46

CHIPPING SODBURY

M4

B4066

A38

M4

M5

BRISTOL

BERKELEY CASTLE

0   3   6   9   12
Miles

TOUR #3

* HUNTS COURT GARDEN
* WESTONBIRT ARBORETUM
* BERKELEY CASTLE

• TUESDAY THROUGH SATURDAY •

If you are looking for a real variety of garden styles, this may be the tour for you. Start with the 20th Century rose garden at Hunts Court and plan on at least two hours there especially if you like roses as much as I do. Westonbirt Arboretum, from the 19th Century, has a wonderful collection of plants and it's a great place to stop for a picnic. End your day with the 12th Century romance of Berkeley Castle. A minimum of one hour each is needed at Berkeley Castle and Westonbirt. Travel time between Westonbirt Arboretum and Hunts Court and is 20 minutes. Travel time between Westonbirt and Berkeley Castle is 20 minutes.

HUNTS COURT GARDEN

- Hours of Admission: 9:00 to 5:00
- Location: 2 miles northwest of Wotton-under-Edge; from Wotton B4060 Dursley Rd turn right in Nibley at Black Horse Tavern

  - A 20th Century garden, this 2.5 acres with great views was created over the last 20 years by Keith & Margaret Marshall
  - You will find a remarkable collection of 400 varieties of roses including species, albas, damasks, gallicas and bourbons.
  - Numerous trees and shrubs have been planted to complement the roses and the paths meander to give you a quiet, peaceful feeling.
  - The Sundial Garden contains a large collection of penstemons along with many other herbaceous perennials
  - Look for each of the 30 varieties of hardy geraniums and the outstanding collection of 60 shrubby potentillas.
  - There is beauty in all seasons here including the autumn color of the trees.
  - Note: A wonderful nursery to visit even if you can't take anything home. There is a huge selection of roses, most are never seen in the States.

Berkeley Castle looms above the Terraced Garden.

BERKELEY CASTLE

- Hours of Admission: 2:00 to 5:00
- Location: at Town of Berkeley on B4066

  - This formidable castle has been home to the Berkeley family since the 12th century.
  - You will see a garden of simple terraces with grass walks and narrow, low growing borders. Not the color you may see in other gardens but beautiful in its own right.
  - Four levels of terraces are planted with a wide selection of drought tolerant, sun-loving and tender plants.
  - Enjoy the terrific assortment of climbing, wall plants including evergreen magnolias, banksian roses, clematis and a wisteria that rises the whole height of the castle.
  - There is also a lovely formal lily pond.
  - Note: A "Robin Hood" castle in excellent condition, it conveys a wonderful touch of medieval romance.

■■

WESTONBIRT ARBORETUM

- Hours of Admission: 10:00 to 8:00
- Location: 3.5 miles southwest of Tetbury on A433

- This arboretum, begun in 1829 by Robert Holford, contains many extraordinary specimen trees, some that are quite rare.
- Many new conifers such as the Douglas fir, noble fir, coast redwood and sequoia were imported from North America during the 19th century.
- If you visit in the spring, the collection of ornamental cherries and the wonderful assortment of rhododendrons, azaleas, primroses, wood anemones & bluebells will provide a distinctive mixture of soft shades of blues, pinks and purples.
- Or, if you choose to visit in the fall, the vibrant shades of reds, oranges and yellows will tumble from the large collection of trees.
- Note: Great picnic grounds, good place for a rest in the midst of your travels.

Lovely Walled Garden
At Westbury Court .
(See Tour 1)

OTHER GARDENS IN THE AREA: MISERDEN PARK, PAINSWICK ROCOCO GARDEN, WESTBURY COURT GARDEN

■■

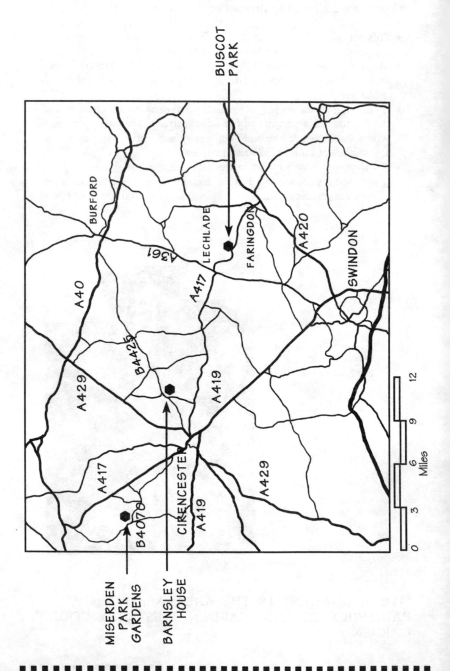

TOUR #4

* MISARDEN PARK GARDENS
* BARNSLEY HOUSE
* BUSCOT PARK

• WEDNESDAY & THURSDAY •

There is a lot to see here! There are wonderful borders everywhere, a famous water feature at Buscot and one of the best known gardens in Britain at Barnsley House. A fair amount of walking is required, plan on approximately two hours for your visit to each garden. Travel time between Misarden and Barnsley House is 20 minutes. Travel time between Barnsley House and Buscot Park is 25 minutes.

MISARDEN PARK GARDENS
- Hours of Admission: 9:30 to 4:30
- Location: 6 miles northwest of Circencester follow the signs off the A417

- This beautiful house stands high overlooking Golden Valley and provides great, panoramic views.
- A wonderful example of the use of land on a hillside. The house sits on a broad cut terrace and the terracing and sloping away of different gardens creates spectacular spaces and marvelous vistas.
- The original house was built in 1620 by Sir William Sandys but it has been somewhat altered by several owners since the early 19th century.
- The walled garden is one of the prettiest I've ever seen. You will find a double border of herbaceous plants facing two additional borders and creating a riot of color.
- A narrow grass path is edged by yew hedges clipped into domes on top, well done.
- The formal rose garden has been newly replanted.
- You will also see a lovely gate house and a quaint old church.

Manor House at
Misarden Park

BARNSLEY HOUSE

- Hours of Admission: 10:00 to 6:00
- Location: 4 miles northeast of Cirencester on B4425

  - One of the best known gardens in Britain and created by one of England's best loved gardeners, Rosemary Verey.
  - You will see a 17th century gabled house that was previously a rectory, a stone wall that was built in 1771 and perimeter trees that were planted in 1840. Work on the four acre garden you see today did not begin until the early 1960's.
  - Mrs. Verey is a great experimenter and each part of garden has its own character. She has used her knowledge of garden history to plan and plant many areas of the garden in historical styles.
  - The many garden styles are blended well. There is the very formal knot garden, planted in 1975, and in contrast, there is the "wilderness" area planted with ornate trees.
  - Look for the much photographed laburnum tunnel; it is truly wonderful, especially in early June.
  - Borders are a collection of plants selected for their shape, color, scent and year-round interest.
  - You will find an eighteen century Tuscan temple with a goldfish pond, the feeling is very peaceful.
  - Intricate potager beds mix roses and clematis with fruits and vegetables.
  - Interesting old sculptures by Simon Verity, such as "Lady with Basket" and "Victorian Woman", are scattered throughout.
  - This is the kind of garden that all of us serious gardeners would like to create and enjoy.

Take a few moments to relax and enjoy your surroundings in the Stone Garden House at Barnsley.

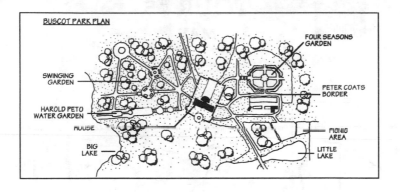

BUSCOT PARK PLAN

FOUR SEASONS GARDEN

SWINGING GARDEN

PETER COATS BORDER

HAROLD PETO WATER GARDEN

HOUSE

PICNIC AREA

BIG LAKE

LITTLE LAKE

BUSCOT PARK (N.T.)

- Hours of admission: 2:00 to 6:00
- Location: 2.5 miles northwest of Faringdon on A417
  - This 18th century house is surrounded by a parkland garden and classic brick walls that provide a perfect background for the flower beds and climbing roses.
  - The house is on a hill with vistas in all directions, vistas that are even more beautiful than the descriptions I read in the picture books.
  - As you enter the garden you see the Peter Coats border. It is two sided with barberries, fuchsia leafed mock orange, six hill giant catmint, peonies, roses and many more. The contrasts in color and shape are lovely and quite different.
  - One of the dominant elements of the design is the famous Harold Peto formal water garden. It is narrow with clipped hedges on either side and water that drops gently through a system of canals and pools and leads your eye from the house, across the lake, to a temple on the far side.
  - Look for the double row of pleached hornbeam trees that form an allee that directs the eye to one of the wonderful views.
  - One very interesting feature is the "swing" garden. This is a place to stop, relax and enjoy the view on a swing built for two.
  - This National Trust property is administered by Lord Faringdon.

OTHER GARDENS IN THE AREA: HUNTS COURT, PUSEY, WESTBURY COURT GARDEN

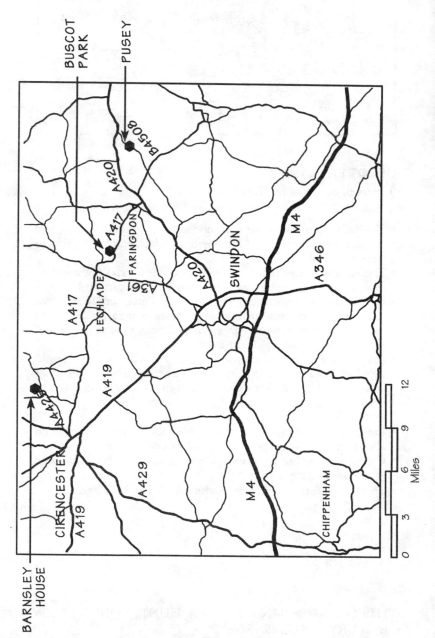

TOUR #5

* BARNSLEY HOUSE
* BUSCOT PARK
* PUSEY

• WEDNESDAY & THURSDAY •

Lots of color and lots to see! Wonderful views and a famous water garden will be found at Buscot Park and Pusey has a 150 foot border that is just fantastic. If you are lucky, Mrs. Verey will be around to greet you at Barnsley House. Plan on approximately two hours for your visit to each garden. Please note that both Buscot Park and Pusey open at 2:00. Travel time between Barnsley House and Buscot Park is 25 minutes. Travel time between Buscot Park and Pusey is 20 minutes.

BARNSLEY HOUSE

- Hours of Admission: 10:00 to 6:00
- Location: 4 miles northeast of Cirencester on B4425

  - One of the best known gardens in Britain and created by one of England's best loved gardeners, Rosemary Verey.
  - You will see a 17th century gabled house that was previously a rectory, a stone wall that was built in 1771 and perimeter trees that were planted in 1840. Work on the four acre garden you see today did not begin until the early 1960's.
  - Mrs. Verey is a great experimenter and each part of garden has its own character. She has used her knowledge of garden history to plan and plant many areas of the garden in historical styles.
  - The many garden styles are blended well. There is the very formal knot garden, planted in 1975, and in contrast, there is the "wilderness" area planted with ornate trees.
  - Look for the much photographed laburnum tunnel, it is truly wonderful, especially in early June.
  - Borders are a collection of plants selected for their shape, color, scent and year-round interest.
  - You will find an eighteen century Tuscan temple with a goldfish pond, the feeling is very peaceful.
  - Intricate potager beds mix roses and clematis with fruits and vegetables.
  - Interesting old sculptures by Simon Verity, such as "Lady with Basket" and "Victorian Woman", are scattered throughout.
  - This is the kind of garden that all of us serious gardeners would like to create and enjoy.

One of
Rosemary Verey's
lovely borders at
Barnsley House.

BUSCOT PARK (N.T.)

- Hours of Admission: 2:00 to 6:00
- Location: 2.5 miles northwest of Faringdon on A417

- This 18th century house is surrounded by a parkland garden and classic brick walls that provide a perfect background for the flower beds and climbing roses.
- The house is on a hill with vistas in all directions, vistas that are even more beautiful than the descriptions I read in the picture books.
- As you enter the garden you see the Peter Coats border. It is two sided with barberries, fuchsia leafed mock orange, six hill giant catmint, peonies, roses and many more. The contrasts in color and shape are lovely and quite different.
- One of the dominant elements of the design is the famous Harold Peto formal water garden. It is narrow with clipped hedges on either side and water that drops gently through a system of canals and pools and leads your eye from the house, across the lake, to a temple on the far side.
- Look for the double row of pleached hornbeam trees that form an allee that directs the eye to one of the wonderful views.
- One very interesting feature is the "swing" garden. This is a place to stop, relax and enjoy the view on a swing built for two.

Harold Peto's famous water
garden at Buscot Park.

Unique
Oriental inspired
bridge at Pusey.

PUSEY
- Hours of Admission: 2:00 to 6:00
- Location: 10 miles southwest of Oxford on A420 turn south onto B4508

  - A charming garden with Cotswold stone walls, big old trees, and exceptional herbaceous borders. The main border is 150 yards long and considered one of the most impressive in England (primary color is blue).
  - The stone house was built in 1748 but gardens were created much more recently by Geoffrey Jellicoe who began refurbishing and creating the grounds in 1937.
  - You enter through a side gate and are greeted by two colorful borders. You continue on and pass through the iron gate at the end of the path and discover a full panoramic view of the garden.
  - A unique Oriental inspired bridge built in 1755 crosses a lovely lake with swans, ducks, fish and water lilies. The bridge has strong horizontal lines, diagonal bracing and crisp white paint.
  - From the lake you look back to spreading lawn leading up to the manor house and lovely terraced beds filled with flowers and many shrub roses.
  - Lady Emily's Garden is a small secluded garden planted mainly with roses. Clematis, hydrangeas and roses cover the brick walls.
  - A private home with a truly wonderful garden.

OTHER GARDENS IN THE AREA: MISERDEN PARK, WESTONBIRT ARBORETUM

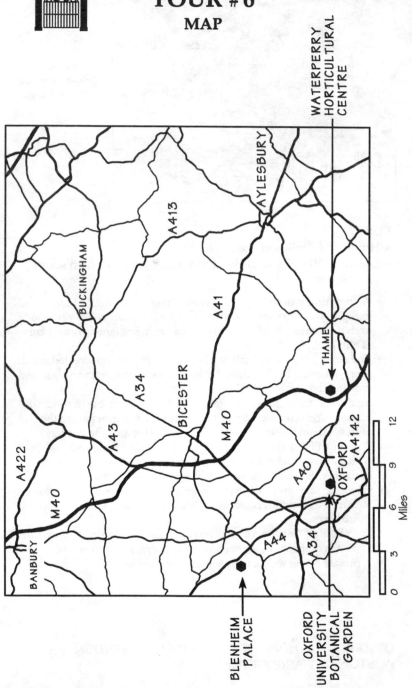

TOUR # 6

* OXFORD UNIVERSITY BOTANIC GARDENS
* WATERPERRY HORTICULTURAL CENTRE
* BLENHEIM PALACE

• DAILY •

Oxford Botanic Garden is a peaceful way to start your day and you will find that the garden and nursery at Waterperry are fun to wander in and enjoy. In contrast Blenheim Palace is an historic garden touched by many of Englands great designers. It is the birthplace of Winston Churchill and a great place for a picnic or for tea overlooking the fabulous fountains. Plan two to three hours at Blenheim especially if you want to see the palace. Plan on approximately two hours each for your visit to Waterperry and Oxford Botanic. Travel time between Oxford Botanic and Waterperry Centre is 20 minutes. Travel time between Waterperry Centre and Blenheim Palace is 40 minutes.

OXFORD UNIVERSITY BOTANIC GARDENS
• Hours of admission: 8:30 to 5:00
• Location: in town center off High St.; entrance opposite
  Magdalen College in Rose Lane.

  • Founded in 1621, this is the oldest botanical garden in Britain, second oldest in Europe.
  • There are 300 species and varieties of wall plants, many quite rare.
  • Near the Lily Pond is Jacob Bobart's yew, probably planted in 1650 (oldest tree in the garden). You will also find a 120 year old Magnolia grandiflora just inside the garden and, in the Walled Garden, there is a great Pinus nigra (black pine) planted in 1800 and believed to be the oldest in Britain.
  • Look for the demonstration bed of historical roses which illustrates the origin of garden roses.
  • The glass houses were rebuilt in 1970 and contain a wide range of tropical and ornamental plants.
  • Spring flowering is exceptional with bearded irises, peonies, poppies and perennials.
  • The flower beds are formal in their layout but informal in planting.
  • This garden is beautifully maintained and conveys a quiet, peaceful feeling amid the hub-bub of this historic college town.
  • Should not be missed especially if you are staying near Oxford, a good place to start several of these tours.

BLENHEIM PALACE

- Hours of Admission: 10:30 to 5:30
- Location: 9 miles northwest of Oxford on A44

  - First Duke of Marborough, John Churchill, built this estate in 1705-1719. The architect was Sir John Vanbrugh and Henry Wise (Queen Anne's gardener) designed the formal gardens.
  - The entire estate is 11,000 acres including the Park (2100 acres) which is surrounded by a 9 mile long dry set stone wall.
  - Enjoy the long drive leading to the palace, you will find sheep grazing freely on either side (they do a good job keeping the grass down).
  - Several great "garden makers" placed their stamp on this estate.
  - Wise devised formal, intricate parterres and a large kitchen garden.
  - Vanbrugh constructed a grand bridge over the River Glyme that became a part of "Capability" Brown's design several years later.
  - Brown arrived in 1764 and swept away most of the formal gardens created by Wise and Vanbrugh when he created the park that now surrounds the palace. He dammed the River Glyme at its south end to create the two lakes you see.
  - French designer Achille Duchene came in the 1920's and created the elegant Italian garden and water terraces adorned with statues and ornamental masonry.
  - This Italian garden is quite lovely with clipped hedges creating a maze, pots of colorful flowers such as geraniums and fuchsias and a fountain with magnificent gilded dolphins.
  - Look for the rose garden. The design is formal and quite different with small beds separated by lawn. Water sounds echo from the circular fountain located in the center and climbing roses reach out and cover the iron fence that encloses the garden.
  - The spring woodland garden is frequently overlooked but is one of the most delightful areas with lovely vistas of flowers such as rare hydrangeas, blue poppies and azaleas and rhododendrons.
  - This was the birthplace of Winston Churchill in 1874.
  - A restaurant looks out to the knot garden and a series of formal fountains (great scones).
  - Note: A great place for a picnic, you can dine with the cows and sheep and swans. If you can, avoid weekends. Your visit requires a fair amount of walking. Take the time to see the palace.

Water Garden at Blenheim Palace

Bright red poppies flourish in the border at Waterperry Centre.

WATERPERRY HORTICULTURAL CENTRE

- Hours of Admission: 10:00 to 6:00
- Location: 6 miles east of Oxford on A40; turn northeast at Holton to Waterperry
  - Your first impression is that this is just a garden center with a nice selection of plants and garden pottery but if you look a little deeper, you will find 83 acres of wonderful walled gardens and demonstration beds.
  - A house has been on this site for over 900 years since the Domesday book was written and there is also a Saxon church on the property.
  - The gardens grew out of a horticultural college for young ladies founded in the 1930's by a Miss Havergal.
  - Open grassy areas weave through planting beds and almost 100 yards of magnificent herbaceous perennial borders backed by red brick walls. These plants are selected for their foliage contrasts as well as for color.
  - The rock garden includes many perennials with a surprising array of colors and the alpine area contains the national collection of porophyllum saxifrages.
  - For an interesting effect espaliered fruit trees have been used to separate rows of vegetables in the kitchen garden.
  - A dell and bridge lead to the River Thame, a tributary of the Thames.
  - Note: There are many interesting pieces of pottery, you might be able to find a distributor back home.

OTHER GARDENS IN THE AREA: PUSEY, ROUSHAM PARK, STOWE LANDSCAPE GARDEN. WADDESDON MANOR

TOUR #7
MAP

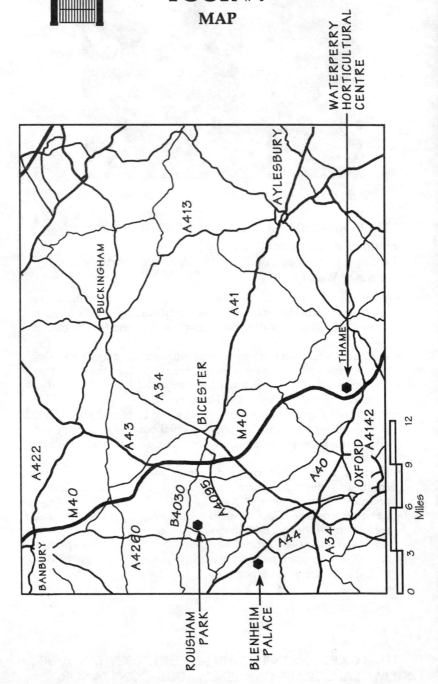

TOUR #7

* WATERPERRY HORTICULTURAL CENTRE
* BLENHEIM PALACE
* ROUSHAM PARK

• DAILY •

Take time to see the palace at Blenheim and you might want to stay for lunch or tea overlooking the fabulous fountains (great scones). Plan on two to three hours for Blenheim Palace. The nursery at Waterperry is fun to wander around in and the garden is really special. Rousham is an important historical park and will give you a chance to meet a few peacocks. Plan on up to two hours each for your visit to Waterperry and Rousham. Travel time between Waterperry Centre and Blenheim Palace is 40 minutes. Travel time between Blenheim Palace and Rousham Park is 20 minutes.

WATERPERRY HORTICULTURAL CENTRE

- Hours of Admission: 10:00 to 6:00
- Location: 6 miles east of Oxford on A40; turn northeast at Holton to Waterperry

- Your first impression is that this is just a garden center with a nice selection of plants and garden pottery but if you look a little deeper, you will find 83 acres of wonderful walled gardens and demonstration beds.
- A house has been on this site for over 900 years since the Domesday book was written and there is also a Saxon church on the property.
- The gardens grew out of a horticultural college for young ladies founded in the 1930's by a Miss Havergal.
- Open grassy areas weave through planting beds and almost 100 yards of magnificent herbaceous perennial borders backed by red brick walls. These plants are selected for their foliage contrasts as well as for color.
- The rock garden includes many perennials with a surprising array of colors and the alpine area contains the national collection of porophyllum saxifrages.
- For an interesting effect espaliered fruit trees have been used to separate rows of vegetables in the kitchen garden.
- A dell and bridge lead to the River Thame, a tributary of the Thames.
- Note: There are many interesting pieces of pottery, you might be able to find a distributor back home.

BLENHEIM PALACE

- Hours of admission: 10:30 to 5:30
- Location: 9 miles northwest of Oxford on A44

- First Duke of Marborough, John Churchill, built this estate in 1705-1719. The architect was Sir John Vanbrugh and Henry Wise (Queen Anne's gardener) designed the formal gardens.
- The entire estate is 11,000 acres including the Park (2100 acres) which is surrounded by a 9 mile long dry set stone wall.
- Enjoy the long drive leading to the palace, you will find sheep grazing freely on either side (they do a good job keeping the grass down).
- Several great "garden makers" placed their stamp on this estate.
- Wise devised formal, intricate parterres and a large kitchen garden.
- Vanbrugh constructed a grand bridge over the River Glyme that became a part of "Capability" Brown's design several years later.
- Brown arrived in 1764 and swept away most of the formal gardens created by Wise and Vanbrugh when he created the park that now surrounds the palace. He dammed the River Glyme at it's south end to create the two lakes you see.
- French designer Achille Duchene came in the 1920's and created the elegant Italian garden and water terraces adorned with statues and ornamental masonry.
- This Italian garden is quite lovely with clipped hedges creating a maze, pots of colorful flowers such as geraniums and fuchsias and a fountain with magnificent gilded dolphins.
- Look for the rose garden. The design is formal and quite different with small beds separated by lawn. Water sounds echo from the circular fountain located in the center and climbing roses reach out and cover the iron fence that encloses it.

- The spring woodland garden is frequently overlooked but is one of the most delightful areas with lovely vistas of flowers such as rare hydrangeas, blue poppies and azaleas and rhododendrons.
- This was the birthplace of Winston Churchill in 1874.
- A restaurant looks out to the knot garden and a series of formal fountains (great scones).
- Note: A great place for a picnic, you can dine with the cows and sheep and swans. If you can, avoid weekends. Your visit requires a fair amount of walking. Take the time to see the palace.

Wisteria provides a wonderful background for this classic sculpture at Blenheim.

An interesting effect is created by boxwood hedges surrounding the rose beds at Rousham Park.

ROUSHAM PARK

- Hours of Admission: 10:00 to 4:30
- Location: 14 miles north of Oxford on A4260 turn east

  - Historically important and a delight to any visitor, this estate is a perfect example of an English landscape park of the early 18th century. The setting is the River Cherwell and its valley.
  - Created by William Kent in 1737-41 out of earlier layout by Charles Bridgeman, it remains almost as it was and is one of the few gardens of this date to have escaped alteration.
  - In addition to the manor house, there is a small church that was built in 1214.
  - The grounds that surround the manor are very plain but as you pass through a beautiful iron gate you enter a lovely brick walled garden with roses, peonies and colorful perennials.
  - A series of garden rooms are defined by either brick walls, trees or shrubs. Look for the peacocks, they roam freely through the garden.
  - You will find a glorious statue of a lion attacking a horse by Dutch sculptor Pieter Scheemaker.
  - If you are willing to take a longer walk, the Cold Bath with its elaborate waterways, the seven-arched arcades or portico and the gentle cascades in Venus Vale, where great carp swim lazily, are all wonderful.
  - Note: If you do not have correct change for the entrance fee, someone in the garden will collect it. Children under 15 are not allowed.

OTHER GARDENS IN THE AREA: OXFORD UNIVERSITY BOTANIC GARDEN, PUSEY, STOWE LANDSCAPE GARDEN, WADDESDON MANOR

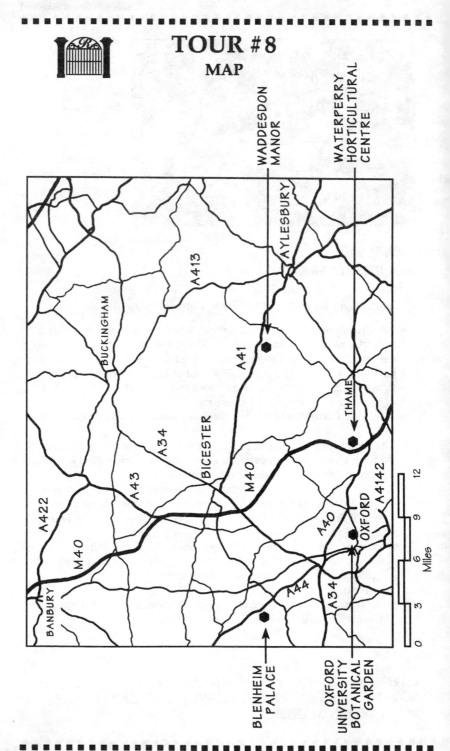

TOUR #8
MAP

TOUR #8

* WATERPERRY HORTICULTURAL CENTRE
* BLENHEIM PALACE
* WADDESDON MANOR
* OXFORD UNIVERSITY BOTANIC GARDENS

• WEDNESDAY THROUGH SUNDAY •

This is really a full day, no time to dawdle! Spend at least an hour in the garden and nursery at Waterperry. Then plan on a picnic during your visit at Blenheim Palace. You will need two to three hours to properly enjoy Blenheim especially if you want to see the palace itself. End the day with the Rothschields at Waddesdon, the garden, the house and the aviary are all grand. Plan on up to two hours at Waddesdon. Remember, if you want to start bright and early Oxford Botanic opens at 8:30. Travel time between Oxford Botanic and Waterperry Centre is 20 minutes. Travel time between Waterperry Centre and Blenheim Palace is 40 minutes. Travel time between Blenheim Palace and Waddesdon Manor is 60 minutes.

WATERPERRY HORTICULTURAL CENTRE

- Hours of Admission: 10:00 to 6:00
- Location: 6 miles east of Oxford on A40; turn northeast at Holton to Waterperry

  - Your first impression is that this is just a garden center with a nice selection of plants and garden pottery but if you look a little deeper, you will find   83 acres of wonderful walled gardens and demonstration beds.
  - A house has been on this site for over 900 years since the Domesday book was written and there is also a Saxon church on the property.
  - The gardens grew out of a horticultural college for young ladies founded in the 1930's by a Miss Havergal.
  - Open grassy areas weave through planting beds and almost 100 yards of magnificent herbaceous perennial borders backed by red brick walls. These plants are selected for their foliage contrasts as well as for color.
  - The rock garden includes many perennials with a surprising array of colors and the alpine area contains the national collection of porophyllum saxifrages.
  - For an interesting effect espaliered fruit trees have been used to separate rows of vegetables in the kitchen garden.
  - A dell and bridge lead to the River Thame, a tributary of the Thames.
  - Note: There are many interesting pieces of pottery, you might be able to find a distributor back home.

BLENHEIM PALACE

- Hours of Admission: 10:30 to 5:30
- Location: 9 miles northwest of Oxford on A44

  - First Duke of Marborough, John Churchill, built this estate in 1705-1719. The architect was Sir John Vanbrugh and Henry Wise (Queen Anne's gardener) designed the formal gardens.
  - The entire estate is 11,000 acres including the Park (2100 acres) which is surrounded by a 9 mile long dry set stone wall.
  - Enjoy the long drive leading to the palace, you will find sheep grazing freely on either side (they do a good job keeping the grass down).
  - Several great "garden makers" placed their stamp on this estate.
  - Wise devised formal, intricate parterres and a large kitchen garden.
  - Vanbrugh constructed a grand bridge over the River Glyme that became a part of "Capability" Brown's design several years later.
  - Brown arrived in 1764 and swept away most of the formal gardens created by Wise and Vanbrugh when he created the park that now surrounds the palace. He dammed the River Glyme at its south end to create the two lakes you see.
  - French designer Achille Duchene came in the 1920's and created the elegant Italian garden and water terraces adorned with statues and ornamental masonry.
  - This Italian garden is quite lovely with clipped hedges creating a maze, pots of colorful flowers such as geraniums and fuchsias and a fountain with magnificent gilded dolphins.
  - Look for the rose garden. The design is formal and quite different with small beds separated by lawn. Water sounds echo from the circular fountain located in the center and climbing roses reach out and cover the iron fence that encloses the garden.
  - The spring woodland garden is frequently overlooked but is one of the most delightful areas with lovely vistas of flowers such as rare hydrangeas, blue poppies and azaleas and rhododendrons.
  - This was the birthplace of Winston Churchill in 1874.
  - A restaurant looks out to the knot garden and a series of formal fountains (great scones).
  - Note: A great place for a picnic, you can dine with the cows and sheep and swans. If you can, avoid weekends. Your visit requires a fair amount of walking. Take the time to see the palace.

Water Garden & Cafe at Blenheim Palace.

■■■

WADDESDON MANOR (N.T.)

- Hours of Admission: 11:00 to 5:00
- Location: 6 miles northwest of Aylesbury on A41
  - Baron Ferdinand de Rothschield began construction of the house and the reshaping of the grounds in 1874. Located on a hill, the manor house has magnificent views.
  - Elie Laine, a Parisian, was the landscape architect, but the planting was anything but French. Instead, the large groupings of colorful trees are a good example of the new trend of the period toward color.
  - A partnership between the Rothschield family and the National Trust undertook the restoration beginning in 1989 and it was decided to return the grounds as nearly as possible to its original state.
  - The garden sculptures collected by Baron Ferdinand are 18th century Italian & Dutch. They still occupy their original positions and are unrivaled as a collection in Britain.
  - The centerpiece of the south facing terrace is the fountain, an early 18th century group of Pluto and Proserpine by Giuliano Mozani.
  - The original Parterre, a mixture of carpet bedding and large masses of pelargoniums and begonias, contained 50,000 plants at the turn of the century.
  - Beth Rothschield drew the design for the new parterre. Her aim was to restore the effect of the turn-of-the-century bedding. A total of 25,000 permanent and summer plants were used in 1993.
  - The Aviary, in the Rococo style, was completed in 1889.
  - Many new trees had to be planted to restore the original masses.

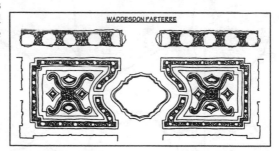

New Parterre at Waddesdon.

OXFORD UNIVERSITY BOTANIC GARDENS

- Hours of Admission: 8:30 to 5:00
- Location: in town center off High St.; entrance opposite Magdalen College in Rose Lane.

For more information on this garden, see Tour 6 and page 106 under "Garden Descriptions".

OTHER GARDENS IN THE AREA: PUSEY, ROUSHAM PARK, STOWE LANDSCAPE GARDEN

■■■

TOUR #9
MAP

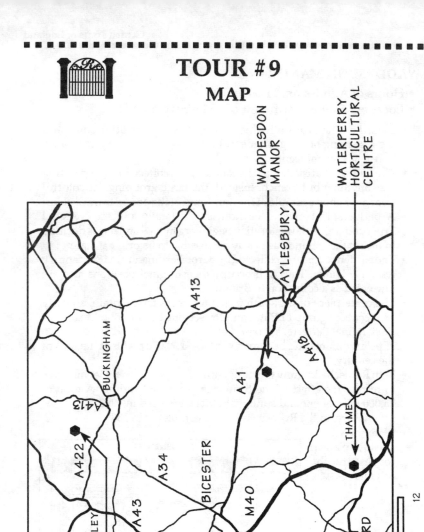

WADDESDON MANOR

WATERPERRY HORTICULTURAL CENTRE

AYLESBURY

A413

BUCKINGHAM

A41

A418

A413

THAME

A422

A34

BICESTER

M40

BRACKLEY

A43

M40

A40

OXFORD

A44

A34

BANBURY

STOWE LANDSCAPE GARDEN

Miles

0   3   6   9   12

46

TOUR #9

* STOWE LANDSCAPE GARDEN
* WADDESDON MANOR
* WATERPERRY HORTICULTURAL CENTRE

• WEDNESDAY, FRIDAY, SUNDAY •

Plan on a couple hours and a fair amount of walking at Stowe if you want to really see this historic garden. Next visit the Rothschield family at Waddesdon, the garden sculptures rival the art collection in the house. Finish the day by having fun wandering around the wonderful garden and nursery at Waterperry. Plan on approximately two hours each at Waddesdon and Waterperry. Travel time between Stowe and Waddesdon Manor is 60 minutes. Travel time between Waddesdon Manor and Waterperry Centre is 40 minutes.

STOWE LANDSCAPE GARDEN (N.T.)
* Hours of Admission: 10:00 to 5:00
* Location: 3 miles northwest of Buckingham off A422

  * This may be the most important landscape garden in Britain. It is one of the supreme creations of the Georgian era.
  * Initially formal in design, Sir Richard Temple (Viscount Cobham) began construction in the 16th century. It took 40 years and a great deal of money to achieve his goal.
  * In the 18th century the Temple family employed many leading architects, landscape architects and sculptors. Vanbrugh, Bridgeman, Kent and Brown were all involved in designing the garden.
  * Between 1714 and 1720 Charles Bridgeman laid out formal gardens to the south of the house.
  * See if you can find the 30 garden buildings (temples, obelisks, a grotto and a shell bridge) designed by William Kent.
  * One of the most impressive sights is the Elysian Fields which was also designed by William Kent.
  * "Capability" Brown (head gardener from 1741 to 1751), recreated the rolling hills, woods and lakes in the new naturalistic style of the period.
  * Bankruptcy in 1848 forced the sale of the contents of the house and the estate was sold in 1920 and turned into a school.
  * The National Trust acquired the property in 1989 and has embarked on one of the most ambitious and expensive programs of garden restoration ever undertaken in Britain; a restoration that will take more than 10 years.
  * Note: Very interesting and worth seeing but the garden is in the midst of restoration.

William Kent's bridge spans the lake built by "Capability" Brown at Stowe.

WADDESDON MANOR (N.T.)
- Hours of Admission: 11:00 to 5:00
- Location: 6 miles northwest of Aylesbury on A41

- Baron Ferdinand de Rothschield began construction of the house and the reshaping of the grounds in 1874. Located on a hill, the manor house has magnificent views.
- Elie Laine, a Parisian, was the landscape architect, but the planting was anything but French. Instead, the large groupings of colorful trees are a good example of the new trend of the period toward color.
- The National Trust received the house and it's immediate grounds (165 acres) by bequest in 1957.
- A partnership between the Rothschield family and the National Trust undertook the restoration beginning in 1989 and it was decided to return the grounds as nearly as possible to its original state.
- The garden sculptures collected by Baron Ferdinand are 18th century Italian & Dutch. They still occupy their original positions and are unrivaled as a collection in Britain.
- The centerpiece of the south facing terrace is the fountain, an early 18th century group of Pluto and Proserpine by Giuliano Mozani.
- The original Parterre, a mixture of carpet bedding and large masses of pelargoniums and begonias, contained 50,000 plants at the turn of the century.
- Beth Rothschield drew the design for the new parterre. Her aim was to restore the effect of the turn-of-the-century bedding. A total of 25,000 permanent and summer plants were used in 1993.
- The Aviary, in the Rococo style, was completed in 1889.
- Many new trees had to be planted to restore the original masses. Experiments have begun to transplant semi-mature trees into the garden.

The fabulous
18th Century Italian
fountain at
Waddesdon Manor.

WATERPERRY HORTICULTURAL CENTRE
- Hours of Admission: 10:00 to 6:00
- Location: 6 miles east of Oxford on A40; turn northeast at Holton to Waterperry

  - Your first impression is that this is just a garden center with a nice selection of plants and garden pottery but if you look a little deeper, you will find 83 acres of wonderful walled gardens and demonstration beds.
  - A house has been on this site for over 900 years since the Domesday book was written and there is also a Saxon church on the property.
  - The gardens grew out of a horticultural college for young ladies founded in the 1930's by a Miss Havergal.
  - Open grassy areas weave through planting beds and almost 100 yards of magnificent herbaceous perennial borders backed by red brick walls. These plants are selected for their foliage contrasts as well as for color.
  - The rock garden includes many perennials with a surprising array of colors and the alpine area contains the national collection of porophyllum saxifrages.
  - For an interesting effect espaliered fruit trees have been used to separate rows of vegetables in the kitchen garden.
  - A dell and bridge lead to the River Thame, a tributary of the Thames.
  - Note: There are many interesting pieces of pottery, you might be able to find a distributor back home.

OTHER GARDENS IN THE AREA: BLENHEIM PALACE, OXFORD UNIVERSITY BOTANIC GARDEN, ROUSHAM PARK

TOUR #10
MAP

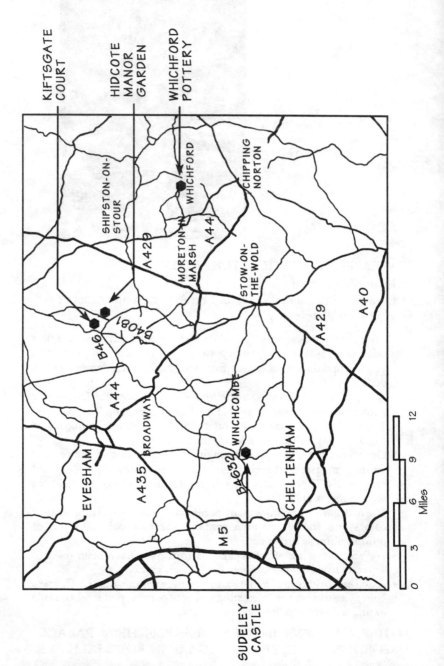

TOUR #10

* SUDELEY CASTLE
* HIDCOTE MANOR
* KIFTSGATE COURT

• WEDNESDAY, THURSDAY, SUNDAY •

A charming and romantic setting, Sudeley Castle is a wonderful way to spend an hour or two. Hidcote and Kiftsgate are right across the road from each other so there is very little travel time which gives you more time to see these fantastic gardens. Hidcote is one of the most famous and influential gardens of this century but Kiftsgate is the kind of garden we'd all like to live with. A minimum of two hours at each of these two gardens. Travel time from Sudeley Castle to Hidcote and Kiftsgate is 30 minutes.

SUDELEY CASTLE
- Hours of admission: 10:30 to 5:30
- Location: 6 miles northeast of Cheltenham on B4632, turn east at Winchcombe

  - This was the home of Queen Katherine Parr (Henry VIII's 6th wife) in the 16th century.
  - The castle is still standing but several other buildings were partially destroyed by Cromwell's troops during the Reformation.
  - Look for the lovely rectangular lily pond that sits in front of the magnificent tithe barn ruins.
  - The walls of these same ruins provide a great backdrop for a wonderful walled garden with roses climbing everywhere.
  - An award winning Tudor rose garden, the Queen's Garden, was laid out by Emma Dent in the mid 19th century and is an imitation of the medieval original. There are hundreds of varieties of old fashioned English roses.
  - The Knot Garden was opened to commemorate the anniversary of Queen Elizabeth I's visit to the castle in 1592. The design was inspired by dress fabric worn by the Queen in a painting hanging in the castle.
  - You will find a number of wonderful hedges that seem to require extensive and continual trimming.
  - Note: The gardens are not spectacular but pretty, charming and very romantic, what a movie set!

Frequently photographed topiaries at Hidcote Manor

HIDCOTE MANOR (N.T.)

- Hours of Admission: 11:00 to 7:00
- Location: 3.5 miles north of Chipping Camden on B4081, turn east at junction with A46

  - One of the great masterpieces of garden design and probably the most influential and famous English garden from this century.
  - Created by an American, Major Lawrence Johnston, who started prior to World War I and continued until his death in 1958.
  - The emphasis on structure was taken from the classical French period of gardening but the planting was English with an enriched color palette.
  - You will find that the design is much like a house with several rooms. A central hall or courtyard opens to garden rooms to the right and left.
  - The tapestry hedge, a mix of yew, box, holly, beech and hornbeam. These hedges were used to create the rooms, a new concept at the time.
  - Look for the famous white garden; it is a mixture of white flowers, silver foliage and clipped box topiaries.
  - One of the most photographed areas is the lily pond, filled with colorful goldfish and surrounded by clipped hedges and topiaries.
  - Johnston personally collected many plants on a plant expedition in Africa and China in 1927. Additionally, many friends sent him plants from all over the world.
  - Several of the plants found here were named after either Johnston or Hidcote itself.
  - This National Trust garden is formal in design and very well maintained.
  - Note: A very famous and popular garden so it can be busy on weekends.

NOTE: Chipping Camden, Lower Slaughter, Stow-on-the-Wold, Broadway, Stanton, Bourton-on-the-Water, just a few of the wonderful little towns in the Cotswolds. Worth visiting for their charm, their thatched roofs, their gardens and the shopping.

KIFTSGATE COURT

- Hours of Admission: 2:00 to 6:00
- Location: 3.5 miles north of Chipping Camden on B4081, turn east at junction with A46

  - Across the lane from Hidcote but what a contrast!
  - The garden was created by Mrs. Heather Muir, grandmother of present owner after World War I. She was assisted by her friend Major Johnston of Hidcote. The garden has changed over the years but the family has stayed true to the ideas and feelings of Mrs. Muir.
  - A 19th century, Georgian style stone house with a great front porch was built in 1887-91.
  - You will find wide borders planted in pinks, purples and crimson with gray foliage, a Rose border, a Yellow border and a White Sunken garden showing the four seasons.
  - There are glorious Japanese maples, wonderful old chestnuts, hedges of Gallica, "Rosa Mundi" and musk, Rosa filipes "Kiftsgate" (flowers in July) cover several trees.
  - Winding walks lead you throughout the garden to the swimming pool lawn, and an octagonal fountain.
  - Look for several pieces of unusual sculpture, they are almost American Indian-like in design.
  - The look is eclectic but with the knowledge that everything is in its proper place.
  - There is something different about this garden. Part of it is that the fantastic, panoramic views become a part of the garden itself.
  - This is a personal creation and cared for with love. A garden for someone's home, which it is.

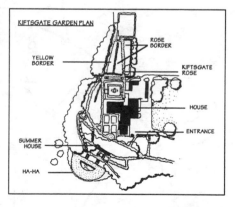

NOTE: There is a wonderful pottery in this area. Whichford Pottery has a team of experienced craftsmen that provides hand made pots for many of the grand manors of the country as well as for private homes. Stop by and see all the wonderful pots and, if you call ahead, they may be able to give you the grand tour. Located in Whichford, near Shipston-on-Stour, Warwickshire, phone (01608) 684416

OTHER GARDENS IN THE AREA: BATSFORD PARK ARBORETUM, BOURTON HOUSE GARDEN, THE PRIORY, SEZINCOTE, SNOWSHILL MANOR

TOUR #11
MAP

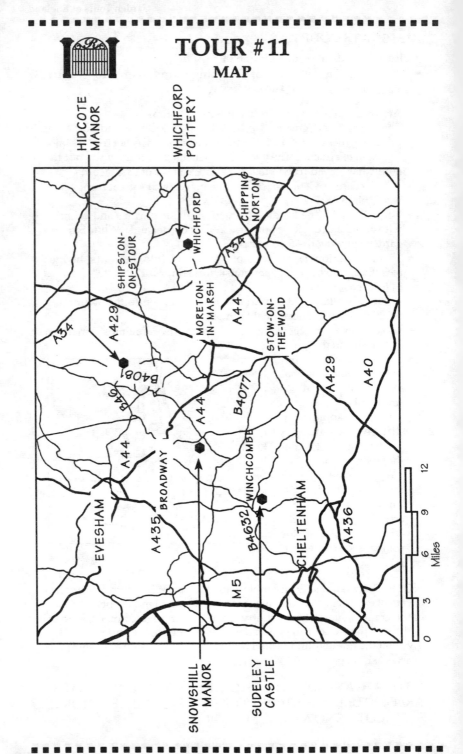

■■■

TOUR #11

* HIDCOTE MANOR
* SUDELEY CASTLE
* SNOWSHILL MANOR

• DAILY EXCEPT TUESDAY AND FRIDAY •

Hidcote is a wonderful garden to be enjoyed and appreciated as one of the most influential gardens of this century. You should plan on up to three hours. A little romance and a lot of history, that is what you will find at the charming Sudeley Castle. The sights and sounds of colorful borders and Chinese wind chimes are the joys of Snowshill Manor. The house is also interesting with its many collections. One to two hours each are needed for Sudeley and Snowshill. Travel time from Hidcote to Sudeley is 30 minutes. Travel time from Sudeley to Snowshill is 20 minutes.

SUDELEY CASTLE
- Hours of Admission: 10:30 to 5:30
- Location: 6 miles northeast of Cheltenham on B4632, turn east at Winchcombe

  - This was the home of Queen Katherine Parr (Henry VIII's 6th wife) in the 16th century.
  - The castle is still standing but several other buildings were partially destroyed by Cromwell's troops during the Reformation.
  - Look for the lovely rectangular lily pond that sits in front of the magnificent tithe barn ruins.
  - The walls of these same ruins provide a great backdrop for a wonderful walled garden with roses climbing everywhere.
  - An award winning Tudor rose garden, the Queen's Garden, was laid out by Emma Dent in the mid 19th century and is an imitation of the medieval original. There are hundreds of varieties of old fashioned English roses.
  - The Knot Garden was opened to commemorate the anniversary of Queen Elizabeth I's visit to the castle in 1592. The design was inspired by dress fabric worn by the Queen in a painting hanging in the castle.
  - You will find a number of wonderful hedges that seem to require extensive and continual trimming.
  - Note: The gardens are not spectacular but pretty, charming and very romantic, what a movie set!

■■

Magnificent tithe barn ruins overlooking lily pond at Sudeley Castle.

HIDCOTE MANOR (N.T.)

- Hours of Admission: 11:00 to 7:00
- Location: 3.5 miles north of Chipping Camden on B4081, turn east at junction with A46

- One of the great masterpieces of garden design and probably the most influential and famous English garden from this century.
- Created by an American, Major Lawrence Johnston, who started prior to World War I and continued until his death in 1958.
- The emphasis on structure was taken from the classical French period of gardening but the planting was English with an enriched color palette.
- You will find that the design is much like a house with several rooms. A central hall or courtyard opens to garden rooms to the right and left.
- There are hedges of every description- yew, copper beech, hornbeam, boxwood and the tapestry hedge, a mix of yew, box, holly, beech and hornbeam. These hedges were used to create the rooms, a new concept at the time.
- Look for the famous white garden; it is a mixture of white flowers, silver foliage and clipped box topiaries.
- One of the most photographed areas is the lily pond, filled with colorful goldfish and surrounded by clipped hedges and topiaries.
- The rose garden has a collection of old shrub roses.
- Johnston personally collected many plants on a plant expedition in Africa and China in 1927. Additionally, many friends sent him plants from all over the world.
  Several of the plants found here were named after either Johnston or Hidcote itself.
- This National Trust garden is formal in design and very well maintained.
- Note: A very famous and popular garden so it can be busy on weekends.

Garden House.

SNOWSHILL MANOR (N.T.)

- Hours of Admission; 1:00 to 6:00
- Location: 3 miles south of Broadway on road to Snowshill

  - This was an old farm that was restored by Arts and Crafts Movement architect Charles Wade about 1920. It is now owned and maintained by the National Trust.
  - You will find that the garden is organized into a series of terraces and outdoor rooms.
  - The style of planting is rather unsophisticated with double borders of mixed flowers, and espalier fruit trees.
  - Well Court is the heart of the garden; you will find a formal lily pond enclosed by walls of climbing roses, clematis and other vines.
  - Look for the contrast of the mauve and blue flowers against the Cotswold stone walls.
  - All the doors, windows and gates are painted an brilliant deep turquoise blue, Wade blue, named after the architect.
  - Sounds are an important part of your experience, listen for a striking clock, Chinese wind chimes and many soft water effects.
  - This garden is lovely all year round but it is best as a garden of summer flowers
  - Note: Take a few minutes to visit the house. Wade was famous for his "heterogeneous assemblage of objects" including musical instruments, clocks and Japanese armor.

Figure of St. George
Slaying the Dragon at
Snowshill Manor.

NOTE: There is a wonderful pottery in this area. Whichford Pottery has a team of experienced craftsmen that provides hand made pots for many of the grand manors of the country as well as for private homes. Stop by and see all the wonderful pots and, if you call ahead, they may be able to give you the grand tour. Located in Whichford, near Shipston-on-Stour, Warwickshire, phone (01608) 684416

NOTE: Chipping Camden, Lower Slaughter, Stow-on-the-Wold, Broadway, Stanton, Bourton-on-the-Water, just a few of the wonderful little towns in the Cotswolds. Worth visiting for their charm, their thatched roofs, their gardens and the shopping.

OTHER GARDENS IN THE AREA: BATSFORD PARK ARBORETUM, BOURTON HOUSE GARDEN, KIFTSGATE COURT, THE PRIORY, SEZINCOTE

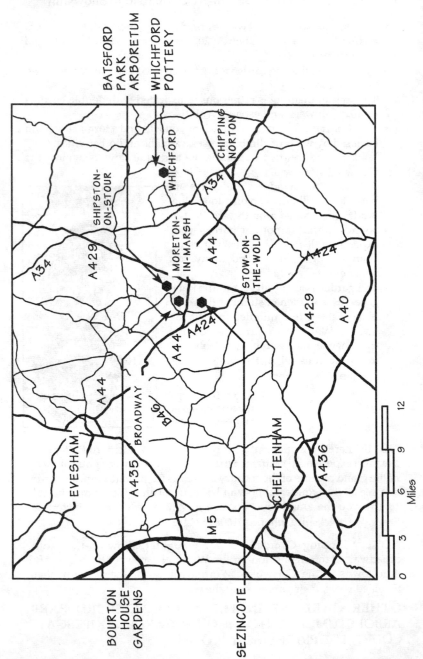

TOUR # 12

* BATSFORD PARK ARBORETUM
* BOURTON HOUSE GARDENS
* SEZINCOTE

• THURSDAY AND FRIDAY •

Batsford Arboretum contains an outstanding collection of plants and several interesting pieces of sculpture and will provide a nice place for a picnic before you continue your tour. I have seen Bourton House develop over the last few years and it is superb. A good example of a formal residential garden with lots of color and shapes. A minimum of one hour each is needed at Batsford and Bourton House. Sezincote is a wonder, interesting and very different with its Middle-Eastern look. A good deal of walking and approximately two hours needed here. Travel time from Batsford to Bourton House is 5 minutes. Travel time from Bourton House to Sezincote is 10 minutes.

BATSFORD PARK ARBORETUM
- Hours of Admission: 10:00 to 5:00
- Location: 5 miles north of Stow-on-the-Wold on A429, turn west at Moreton-in-Marsh

  - The foundation for this arboretum was laid by Lord Redesdale in the 1880's after his return from a post as attaché in the British Embassy in Tokyo. It is distinctly Japanese in an English setting.
  - Redesdale brought back several pieces of sculpture including a large bronze Buddha, a bronze deer and a Chinese dragon.
  - Starting in 1966 Lord Dulverton reclaimed and expanded the arboretum and has greatly increased the number and variety of trees.
  - You will find an outstanding collection of plants, over 1500 named trees & shrubs. You may even find a few varieties you've never seen before.
  - There is much to look at all year round but the best seasons are spring with the flowering magnolias & cherries and fall with the color of Japanese maples, red oaks, beeches and chestnuts.
  - The manor house, built in 1890, replaced an earlier Georgian house. (not open to the public)
  - Note: There is also a garden center and picnic area to enjoy.

Original
bronze
Buddha from
Batsford Park
Arboretum.

BOURTON HOUSE GARDENS
- Hours of Admission: 12:00 to 5:00
- Location: 2 miles west of Moreton-in-Marsh on A44

  - This is a 3 acre residential garden set around a charming manor house (not open). It has been re-established over the last few years and is constantly evolving.
  - As in many formal English gardens, you will find a series of rooms with borders, hedges and a couple of cute Airedales making themselves at home.
  - A marvelous terraced area has a nicely planted borders and a lovely view of the surrounding countryside.
  - You walk into an open lawn area and find it encircled by several beds containing plants that have been combined for their contrasts in foliage color, shape and size. This is truely a plantsmen's paradise.
  - A unique piece of pottery that has been turned into a fountain sits in the middle of an intricate knot garden with boxwood hedges.
  - The tithe barn has been refurbished and appears to be used as a small theater and tea room.
  - Note: I have watched this garden develop over the last few years and it is well worth the visit!

NOTE: There is a wonderful pottery in this area. Whichford Pottery has a team of experienced craftsmen that provides hand made pots for many of the grand manors of the country as well as for private homes. Stop by and see all the wonderful pots and, if you call ahead, they may be able to give you the grand tour. Located in Whichford, near Shipston-on-Stour, Warwickshire, phone (01608) 684416

NOTE: Chipping Camden, Lower Slaughter, Stow-on-the-Wold, Broadway, Stanton, Bourton-on-the-Water, just a few of the wonderful little towns in the Cotswolds. Worth visiting for their charm, their thatched roofs, their gardens and the shopping.

SEZINCOTE

- Hours of Admission: 2:00 to 6:00
- Location: 2 miles west of Moreton-in-Marsh on A44 turn south

  - Xanadu in England. The house is a Hindu-Mongul fantasy in the manner of Akbar with amber walls and a copper dome.
  - As you enter the grounds you will cross a marvelous bridge that is decorated by sacred Brahmin bulls named Nandi, "the happy one".
  - You will see an incredible curving orangery which is possibly the most enticing greenhouse corridor in England.
  - The house was completed in 1805 by Samual Pepys Cockerell for his brother Charles, who had served in the East India Co.
  - Completed in 1810, the garden is more like a park with many mature trees including magnificent cedars of Lebanon.
  - Humphry Repton was consulted on the design of the garden and lakes.
  - The Thornery or water garden and The Temple to Surya, Hindu God of the Sun were designed by Thomas Daniell.
  - The south garden is laid out in Mongul fashion with canals & paths crossing at right angles representing the rivers of life
  - Look for the view of Evenlode Valley, it is the English countryside at its best.
  - Very interesting and completely different from any other place in England.

Sezincote is Xanadu in England.

OTHER GARDENS IN THE AREA: HIDCOTE MANOR GARDEN, KIFTSGATE COURT, THE PRIORY, SNOWSHILL MANOR, SUDELEY CASTLE

TOUR #13
MAP

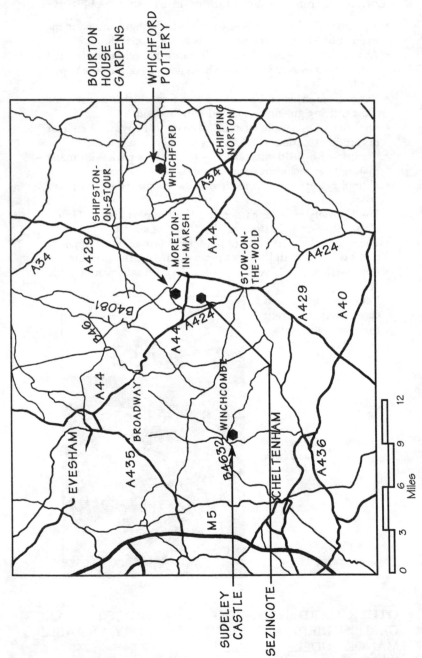

TOUR #13

* SUDELEY CASTLE
* BOURTON HOUSE GARDENS
* SEZINCOTE

• THURSDAY AND FRIDAY •

Remember Henry VIII and Cromwell, if you do you will find history and romance at Sudeley Castle. A favorite of mine, Bourton House has color, form and a few good ideas for your own garden. One to two hours each are needed for Sudeley and Bourton House. Sezincote, a exotic park with an incredible house and orangery. Plan on a fair amount of walking and at least two hours for this trip to the orient. Travel time from Sudeley Castle to Bourton House is 30 minutes. Travel time from Bourton House to Sezincote is 10 minutes.

SUDELEY CASTLE
- Hours of admission: 10:30 to 5:30
- Location: 6 miles northeast of Cheltenham on B4632, turn east at Winchcombe

  - This was the home of Queen Katherine Parr (Henry VIII's 6th wife) in the 16th century.
  - The castle is still standing but several other buildings were partially destroyed by Cromwell's troops during the Reformation.
  - Look for the lovely rectangular lily pond that sits in front of the magnificent tithe barn ruins.
  - The walls of these same ruins provide a great backdrop for a wonderful walled garden with roses climbing everywhere.
  - An award winning Tudor rose garden, the Queen's Garden, was laid out by Emma Dent in the mid 19th century and is an imitation of the medieval original. There are hundreds of varieties of old fashioned English roses.
  - The Knot Garden was opened to commemorate the anniversary of Queen Elizabeth I's visit to the castle in 1592. The design was inspired by dress fabric worn by the Queen in a painting hanging in the castle.
  - You will find a number of wonderful hedges that seem to require extensive and continual trimming.
  - Note: The gardens are not spectacular but pretty, charming and very romantic, what a movie set!

Romantic Sudeley Castle overlooks well clipped yew hedge and rose garden.

BOURTON HOUSE GARDENS

- Hours of Admission: 12:00 to 5:00
- Location: 2 miles west of Moreton-in-Marsh on A44

- This is a 3 acre residential garden set around a charming manor house (not open). It has been re-established over the last few years and is constantly evolving.
- As in many formal English gardens, you will find a series of rooms with borders, hedges and a couple of cute Airedales making themselves at home.
- A marvelous terraced area has a nicely planted borders and a lovely view of the surrounding countryside.
- You walk into an open lawn area and find it encircled by several beds containing plants that have been combined for their contrasts in foliage color, shape and size. This is truly a plantsmen's paradise.
- A unique piece of pottery that has been turned into a fountain sits in the middle of an intricate knot garden with boxwood hedges.
- The tithe barn has been refurbished and appears to be used as a small theater and tea room.
- Note: I have watched this garden develop over the last few years and it is well worth the visit!

One of the colorful borders at Bourton House Gardens.

SEZINCOTE

- Hours of Admission: 2:00 to 6:00
- Location: 2 miles west of Moreton-in-Marsh on A44 turn south

- Xanadu in England. The house is a Hindu-Mongul fantasy in the manner of Akbar with amber walls and a copper dome.
- As you enter the grounds you will cross a marvelous bridge that is decorated by sacred Brahmin bulls named Nandi, "the happy one".
- You will see an incredible curving orangery which is possibly the most enticing greenhouse corridor in England.
- The house was completed in 1805 by Samual Pepys Cockerell for his brother Charles, who had served in the East India Co.
- Completed in 1810, the garden is more like a park with many mature trees including magnificent cedars of Lebanon.
- Humphry Repton was consulted on the design of the garden and lakes.
- The Thornery or water garden and The Temple to Surya, Hindu God of the Sun were designed by Thomas Daniell.
- The south garden is laid out in Mongul fashion with canals & paths crossing at right angles representing the rivers of life
- Look for the view of Evenlode Valley, it is the English countryside at its best.
- Very interesting and completely different from any other place in England.

Across this bridge the fantasy of Sezincote awaits visitors.

NOTE: There is a wonderful pottery in this area. Whichford Pottery has a team of experienced craftsmen that provides hand made pots for many of the grand manors of the country as well as for private homes. Stop by and see all the wonderful pots and, if you call ahead, they may be able to give you the grand tour. Located in Whichford, near Shipston-on-Stour, Warwickshire, phone (01608) 684416

NOTE: Chipping Camden, Lower Slaughter, Stow-on-the-Wold, Broadway, Stanton, Bourton-on-the-Water, just a few of the wonderful little towns in the Cotswolds. Worth visiting for their charm, their thatched roofs, their gardens and the shopping.

OTHER GARDENS IN THE AREA: BATSFORD PARK ARBORETUM, HIDCOTE MANOR GARDEN, KIFTSGATE COURT, THE PRIORY, SNOWSHILL MANOR

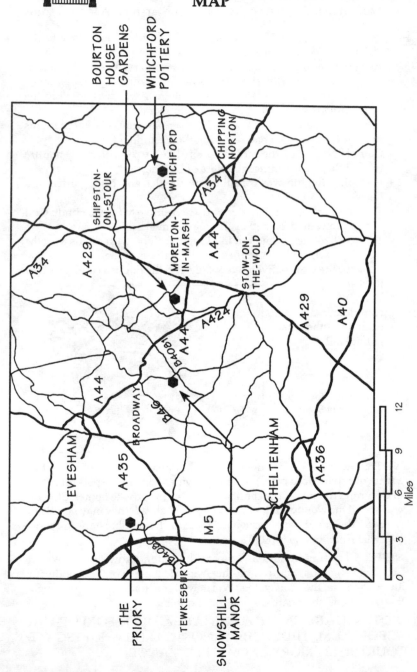

TOUR #14

* BOURTON HOUSE GARDENS
* SNOWSHILL MANOR
* THE PRIORY

• FRIDAY •

This is a good day to relax a little, have a good breakfast, read an English newspaper and see some of the beautiful countryside. Your tour starts at noon and covers three 20th Century gardens. Bourton House, a favorite of mine, is a delightful place that may even give you a few ideas for your own garden. Snowshill is colorful with its mixed borders, "Wade" blue doors and the sounds of several water features. Open only on Fridays, The Priory's lovely borders and yew hedges are well worth waiting for. One to two hours each are needed for these gardens. Travel time from Bourton House to Snowshill is 10 minutes. Travel time from Snowshill to The Priory is 40 minutes.

BOURTON HOUSE GARDENS

- Hours of Admission: 12:00 to 5:00
- Location: 2 miles west of Moreton-in-Marsh on A44

  - This is a 3 acre residential garden set around a charming manor house (not open). It has been re-established over the last few years and is constantly evolving.
  - As in many formal English gardens, you will find a series of rooms with borders, hedges and a couple of cute Airedales making themselves at home.
  - A marvelous terraced area has a nicely planted borders and a lovely view of the surrounding countryside.
  - You walk into an open lawn area and find it encircled by several beds containing plants that have been combined for their contrasts in foliage color, shape and size. This is truly a plantsmen's paradise.
  - A unique piece of pottery that has been turned into a fountain sits in the middle of an intricate knot garden with boxwood hedges.
  - The tithe barn has been refurbished and appears to be used as a small theater and tea room.
  - Note: I have watched this young garden develop over the last few years and it is well worth the visit!

Knot Garden and unusual fountain at Bourton House.

SNOWSHILL MANOR (N.T.)

- Hours of Admission: 1:00 to 6:00
- Location: 3 miles south of Broadway on road to Snowshill

- This was an old farm that was restored by Arts and Crafts Movement architect Charles Wade about 1920. It is now owned and maintained by the National Trust.
- You will find that the garden is organized into a series of terraces and outdoor rooms.
- The style of planting is rather unsophisticated with double borders of mixed flowers, and espalier fruit trees.
- Well Court is the heart of the garden; you will find a formal lily pond enclosed by walls of climbing roses, clematis and other vines.
- Look for the contrast of the mauve and blue flowers against the Cotswold stone walls.
- All the doors, windows and gates are painted an brilliant deep turquoise blue, Wade blue, named after the architect.
- Sounds are an important part of your experience, listen for a striking clock, Chinese wind chimes and many soft water effects.
- This garden is lovely all year round but it is best as a garden of summer flowers
- Note: Take a few minutes to visit the house. Wade was famous for his "heterogeneous assemblage of objects" including musical instruments, clocks and Japanese armor.

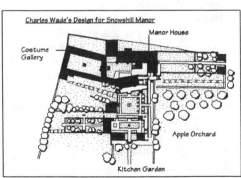

Charles Wade's Design for Snowshill Manor

Manor House

Costume Gallery

Apple Orchard

Kitchen Garden

THE PRIORY
- Hours of Admission: 2:00 to 6:00
- Location: Kemerton, 5 miles northeast of Tewkesbury off B4080

  - This Georgian house, on 4 acres, was taken over by Mr. & Mrs. Peter Healing at the beginning of World War II.
  - Truly a 20th Century garden, the original design was done on pieces of paper during Mr. Healing's wartime service with the RAF. He has made very few changes to that design.
  - Mr. Healing has an eye for design and for a good plant and an obvious love for his garden. You may even find him there, enjoying the day, ready to answer questions and chat.
  - Look for the three lovely mixed and herbaceous borders. One is almost completely red, one has many colors and in the third, the largest (150' long & 19' wide) has colors that range from cool to warm.
  - A yew hedged pastel garden includes perennials, wonderful climbing roses and clematis.
  - Hydrangeas, hostas and peonies fill the sunken garden.
  - See if you can find the huge yew tree dating from the 17th century that is clipped into a giant bun.
  - This is a charming garden with a series of rooms that provide many surprises.

Charming pergola at The Priory.

NOTE: There is a wonderful pottery in this area. Whichford Pottery has a team of experienced craftsmen that provides hand made pots for many of the grand manors of the country as well as for private homes. Stop by and see all the wonderful pots and, if you call ahead, they may be able to give you the grand tour. Located in Whichford, near Shipston-on-Stour, Warwickshire, phone (01608) 684416

NOTE: Chipping Camden, Lower Slaughter, Stow-on-the-Wold, Broadway, Stanton, Bourton-on-the-Water, just a few of the wonderful little towns in the Cotswolds. Worth visiting for their charm, their thatched roofs, their gardens and the shopping.

OTHER GARDENS IN THE AREA: BATSFORD PARK ARBORETUM, HIDCOTE MANOR GARDEN, KIFTSGATE COURT, SEZINCOTE, SUDELEY CASTLE

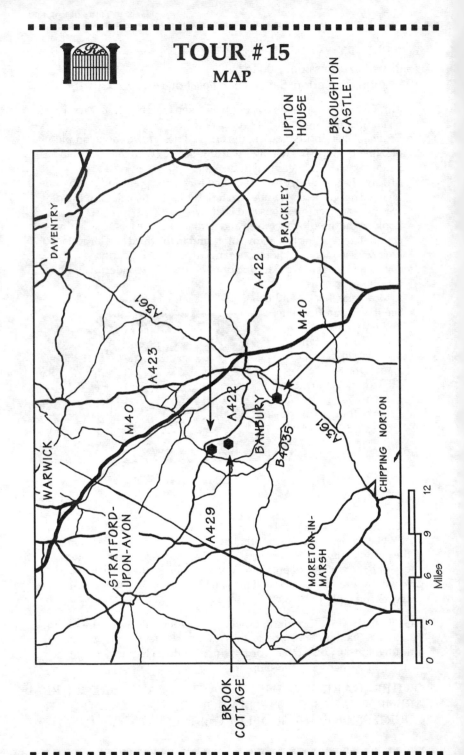

TOUR #15
MAP

UPTON HOUSE

BROUGHTON CASTLE

DAVENTRY

BRACKLEY

A422

A361

M40

A423

M40

A422

BANBURY

WARWICK

B4035

A361

CHIPPING NORTON

STRATFORD-UPON-AVON

A429

MORETON-IN-MARSH

BROOK COTTAGE

0 3 6 9 12
Miles

TOUR #15

* BROOK COTTAGE
* UPTON HOUSE
* BROUGHTON CASTLE

• WEDNESDAY •

Brook Cottage is truly an English garden, with 300 roses and 50 different clematis, it has something to see in all seasons. If you need to inspect each rose like I do, plan on up to two hours. Upton House has a fabulous bog area and lots of surprises in its wonderful terraced gardens. The house also has a fine art collection. Plan on climbing lots of steps and a stay of at least two hours. Glorious countryside, a moated castle and beautiful borders await you at Broughton Castle. At least an hour is needed here. Travel time from Brook Cottage to Upton House is 10 minutes. Travel time from Upton House to Broughton Castle is 20 minutes.

BROOK COTTAGE

- Hours of Admission: 9:00 to 6:00
- Location: 6 miles west of Banbury on A422 turn west toward Alkerton, turn opposite the war memorial

  - Truly an English cottage garden with a funky, lived in look that is tidy and well maintained. It was created almost entirely since 1964 by Mr. & Mrs. David Hodges.
  - In this four acre garden you will find over 300 roses, mostly shrub and climbers; many varieties that are rarely seen in the U.S., and a wonderful display of 50 different varieties of clematis.
  - Areas of lawn follow the natural slope of the land and colorful terraces are filled with varieties of plants, some rarely seen, that are carefully selected for color and contrast.
  - There is a white border that combines white flowers and gray or silver foliage and a yellow border with flowers and foliage in shades of yellow and cream.
  - Look for copper beech hedges surrounding a secret garden, a beautifully planted pool and a tree and shrub area planted with spring bulbs.
  - Mr. & Mrs.Hodges are frequently there to greet you and answer questions. For instance, did you know, it only took 10 or so years for the yew hedge to really look good and, surprisingly, it's trimmed only once a year, in September.
  - Something to see in all seasons from bulbs and flowering cherries in the spring to perennials and roses in the summer to late flowering clematis and autumn color in the fall.

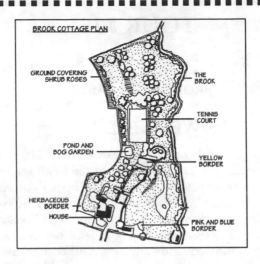

BROOK COTTAGE PLAN

GROUND COVERING
SHRUB ROSES

THE
BROOK

TENNIS
COURT

POND AND
BOG GARDEN

YELLOW
BORDER

HERBACEOUS
BORDER

HOUSE

PINK AND BLUE
BORDER

BROUGHTON CASTLE

- Hours of Admission: 2:00 to 5:00
- Location: 2.5 miles southwest of Banbury on B4035

  - A lovely moated castle built between 1300 and 1550 lies in the midst of a beautiful English pasture.
  - Owned by the same family for over 600 years, it is currently the home of Lord and Lady Saye and Sele.
  - Three acres of open grassy meadows, big old chestnut trees and wonderful borders.
  - A walled garden at the foot of the castle contains flower beds hedged by boxwoods and borders of perennials and shrub roses all in soft pinks, whites and purples. Quite a contrast to the 12th Century castle looming above.
  - One of the more beautiful places in England, especially in June & July.

Knot
Garden
at
Broughton
Castle

UPTON HOUSE (N.T.)

- Hours of Admission: 2:00 to 6:00
- Location: 7 miles northwest of Banbury on A422

  - Sir Rushout Cullen made a major contribution to the original layout of the garden in addition to building the central part of the house in 1695.
  - A major renovation of the house and garden began in 1927. Lord Bearsted worked with architect Morley Horder on the house and wide terraces behind the house and Lady Bearsted with guidance from Kitty Lloyd-Jones created one of Upton's greatest pleasures, its garden.
  - The upper terrace, at the house, is planted with lavender, catmint and old Scots rose "Williams Double Yellow".
  - You are in for quite a surprise here. Standing at the house you look out across a large lawn area which appears to merge with the pasture land in the distance. But step to the edge of the lawn, look down and you will discover an extraordinary terraced garden with brick stairs and big, old trees along the edges.
  - At the bottom is a lake with fountains of grasses and lovely water lilies. Stand at the lake and look back, the house is hidden but the view of the terraces is wonderful.
  - On the terraces you will find "Her Ladyship's Garden", a yew enclosed rose garden with a colorful assortment of flowers, the NCCPG National Collection of asters and fruits & vegetables laid out like a French potager on the warm south slope.
  - The Bog Garden, one of the biggest I've ever seen, is fabulous with its hostas, gunnera, rodgersias along with primulas, astilbes and irises that fill it with luxuriant foliage.
  - Look for the large, traditionally English kitchen garden, the sections of vegetables are divided by rows of fruit bushes.
  - The property was given to the National Trust in 1948.
  - Note: If you can, take the opportunity to visit the house. It contains one of the finest private art collections assembled in England this century.

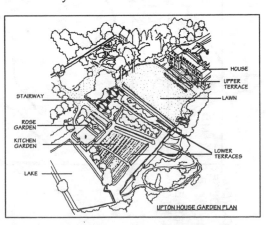

UPTON HOUSE GARDEN PLAN

OTHER GARDENS IN THE AREA: FARNBOROUGH HALL

TOUR #16
MAP

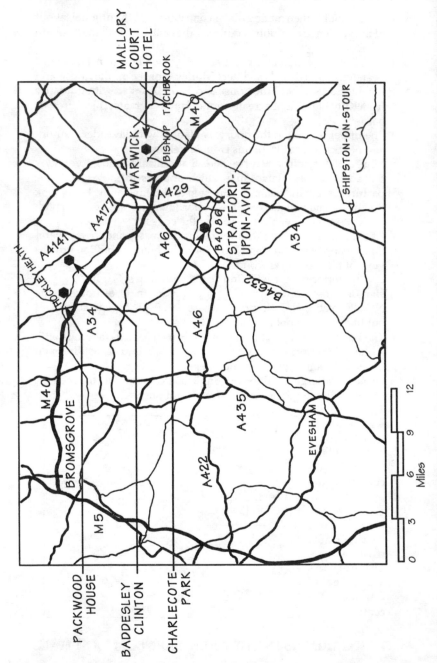

TOUR # 16

* CHARLECOTE PARK
* BADDESLEY CLINTON
* PACKWOOD HOUSE

• FRIDAY, SATURDAY, SUNDAY •

A great house, herds of deer and a formal garden, a place touched by both Will Shakespeare and "Capability" Brown, that's Charlecote Park. At least an hour will be needed here. Baddesley Clinton, I fell in love with this small, moated castle. The grounds are lovely and so is the Norman looking castle. You can see it all in about an hour. One of my absolute favorites is Packwood House. Some of the most wonderful borders and walled gardens and famous clipped yews. I could spend several hours here but you can plan on at least two. Travel time from Charlecote Park to Baddesley Clinton is 30 minutes. Travel time from Baddesley Clinton to Packwood House is 10 minutes.

CHARLECOTE PARK (N.T.)

- Hours of Admission: 11:00 to 6:00
- Location: 4 miles east of Stratford-on-Avon on B4086

- Home of the Lucy family since 1247 and given to National Trust in 1946 along with 180 acres of fenced deer park.
- The house dates from the mid 16th century, but was substantially remodeled in the Elizabethan Revival style in early 19th century. Enjoy all the fru-fru, steeples and stained glass.
- Many of the lovely formal features of the original garden were swept away for the natural look by "Capability" Brown.
- One of the 16th Century features that still remains is a formal garden, with clipped yews, terraces and urns planted with geraniums & lobelia.
- It is said that William Shakespeare poached deer here. To "commemorate" the occasions, a border has been planted with species mentioned in his plays (columbine, dog violets, etc.).
- This is a good example of the care the National Trust takes in refurbishing. The cut out stone walls off the back of the house had deteriorated so badly they had to be replaced. Pictures were used to duplicate the original design in the new stone work, a fantastic job.
- In addition, the knot garden was replanted in its original location. Again an old picture was used to duplicate the original design.
- Approximately 250 Fallow deer roam freely in a preserve seen from the garden. There are black Roman, spotted Menil and 150 Red deer.
- A 19th century orangery is a nice place for tea or lunch.

A moat surrounds the marvelous castle at Baddesley Clinton.

BADDESLEY CLINTON (N.T.)

- Hours of admission: 2:00 to 6:00
- Location: 7.5 miles north of Warwick on A4141

- The history of the property dates back to the 13th century when the Clintons settled and dug the moat. Most of the house, however, is no earlier than the 15th century.
- The home of a lesser English gentry, it lacks the ostentation of the huge estates. The house is unique in its simplicity with a brick bridge entrance over the moat, a gatehouse with gun ports and a facade that has been updated several times over the centuries.
- Lands of smaller gentry were frequently bought up by larger estates so it is rare to find the lands of this estate much as it was described in a survey map of 1699.
- The property was sold several times. The last time was in 1438 to John Brome. His granddaughter married Sir Edward Ferrers whose family held Baddesley until 1939.
- You will note that the forecourt and lovely walled garden remain from early 18th century.
- The Victorian period provided the wooded setting with big, purple rhododendrons.
- Enjoy a peaceful walk around the chain of 15th century fish ponds with swans and water plants.
- The National Trust acquired the property in 1980.
- Note-Take in the whole experience, the natural looking landscape and the marvelous Norman looking castle. It's very simple and very impressive. Well worth the trip.

This bore stands ready to greet you at Charlecote Park.

PACKWOOD HOUSE (N.T.)

- Hours of Admission: 2:00 to 6;00
- Location: 11 miles southeast of central Birmingham on A34 turn east onto B4439 at Hockley Heath

- You will find seven glorious acres of topiaries, borders, walled gardens and some wonderful and unusual details.
- The main block of the house was built in the late 16th Century by the Fetherston family who lived there for nearly 300 years.
- Rising out of the lawn is a remarkable perennial garden with colorful borders and yew hedges surrounding a lovely sunken pool.
- One of the more unusual details is in the rose garden. The bed is backed by a brick wall but the varieties are separated by yew walls.
- Enjoy the elevated double herbaceous border which leads the way from one elevated brick garden house to the other. This section is just gorgeous, very different and provides a glorious view of the garden.
- The austere beauty of the famous yew garden provides an interesting contrast. It was originally set out by John Fetherston c. 1650-1670 is said to represent "The Sermon on the Mount".
- Two Roman baths and the sundials were originally built in 1680.
- Many of the pieces of furniture found in the house where purchased in the 1930's by Baron Ash from nearby Baddesley Clinton. This saved much of the collection. You will also find a wonderful collection of tapestries.
- Mr. Graham Baron Ash, who had spent time and money restoring the house to its original form, gave a total of 113 acres to the National Trust in 1941.

- Note: One of my absolute favorites!

Famous Yew Garden at Packwood House.

NOTE: Mallory Court Hotel, a wonderful place to stay while your touring the area or just a place to visit for its lovely gardens. A charming country hotel has a Michelin-rated restaurant. Located at Bishops Tachbrook, Leamington Spa phone (01926) 330214

OTHER GARDENS IN THE AREA: MILL GARDEN, WARWICK CASTLE

TOUR #17
MAP

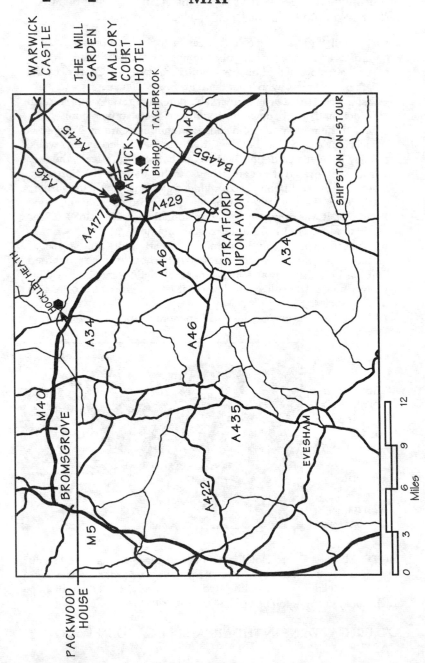

TOUR #17

* THE MILL GARDEN
* WARWICK CASTLE
* PACKWOOD HOUSE

• WEDNESDAY THROUGH SUNDAY •

Before you visit Warwick Castle, stop at the little house and informal gardens on Mill Street. The mood is quiet and reflective with the big old castle looming above. Thirty minutes to an hour is all you need. Warwick Castle, what can I say, this is an event! Plan on three to four hours. A great place to visit after Warwick Castle is Packwood House, one of my favorites. You will see some of the most glorious borders and walled gardens and famous clipped yews. I could spend several hours but you can plan on at least two. Travel time from The Mill Garden to Warwick Castle is maybe five minutes. Travel time from Warwick Castle to Packwood House is 20 minutes.

THE MILL GARDEN
- Hours of Admission: 9:00 to dusk
- Location: beside Warwick Castle, 55 Mill St. (at the end)

  - What a contrast, standing in this lovely, little perennial garden and looking up at that big old castle.
  - Enjoy this cute little house and series of informal garden areas on the river beneath Warwick Castle.
  - You will find the remains of a great old vine covered bridge that once connected to the castle to the far side of the river.
  - The mood is quiet with wonderful water sounds. A good way to start the day and your visit to Warwick.

The cottage garden at Mill Street.

The view from Mill Street Garden up to Warwick Castle.

WARWICK CASTLE

- Hours of Admission: 10:00 to 6:00
- Location: 8 miles northeast of Stratford-on-Avon

- This is an event! Visit for many reasons including the gardens.
- You will find a mediaeval castle with ancient and chivalrous splendor.
- It was originally built by William the Conqueror in 1066 and played a prominent part in English history for 700 years.
- There are 60 acres of grounds and gardens that were landscaped by "Capability" Brown. By the end of the 18th century the gardens had been planted and the castle was basically as we see it today.
- The Victorian rose garden created in 1868 was restored to its original beauty in 1986. It is very formal in design using all old fashion roses.
- Look for the Peacock Garden, a quiet formal garden in front of Conservatory.
- The Pageant Field is a parkland skirted by many fine trees some as old as 200 years.
- Note: This is a popular spot and there are always a lot of people. Admission is a little steep (£8.75) but what an experience!

NOTE: Mallory Court Hotel, wonderful place to stay while your touring the area or just a place to visit for it's lovely gardens. A charming country hotel with a Michelin-rated restaurant. Located at Bishops Tachbrook, Leamington Spa phone (01926) 330214

NOTE: St. Nicholis Park in Warwick is lovely. You might want to stop by for a few minutes while you are in town.

■■

PACKWOOD HOUSE (N.T.)

- Hours of Admission: 2:00 to 6:00
- Location: 11 miles southeast of central Birmingham on A34 turn east onto B4439 at Hockley Heath

  - You will find seven glorious acres of topiaries, borders, walled gardens and some wonderful and unusual details.
  - The main block of the house was built in the late 16th Century by the Fetherston family who lived there for nearly 300 years.
  - Rising out of the lawn is a remarkable perennial garden with colorful borders and yew hedges surrounding a lovely sunken pool.
  - One of the more unusual details is in the rose garden. The bed is backed by a brick wall but the varieties are separated by yew walls.
  - Enjoy the elevated double herbaceous border which leads the way from one elevated brick garden house to the other. This section is just gorgeous, very different and provides a glorious view of the garden.
  - The austere beauty of the famous yew garden provides an interesting contrast. It was originally set out by John Fetherston c. 1650-1670 is said to represent "The Sermon on the Mount".
  - Two Roman baths and the sundials were originally built in 1680.
  - Many of the pieces of furniture found in the house where purchased in the 1930's by Baron Ash from nearby Baddesley Clinton. This saved much of the collection. You will also find a wonderful collection of tapestries.
  - Mr. Graham Baron Ash, who had spent time and money restoring the house to it's original form, gave a total of 113 acres to the National Trust in 1941.
  - Note: One of my absolute favorites!

This colorful perennial garden rises out of the lawn at Packwood House.

OTHER GARDENS IN THE AREA: BADDESLEY CLINTON, CHARLECOTE PARK

■■■

TOUR #18
MAP

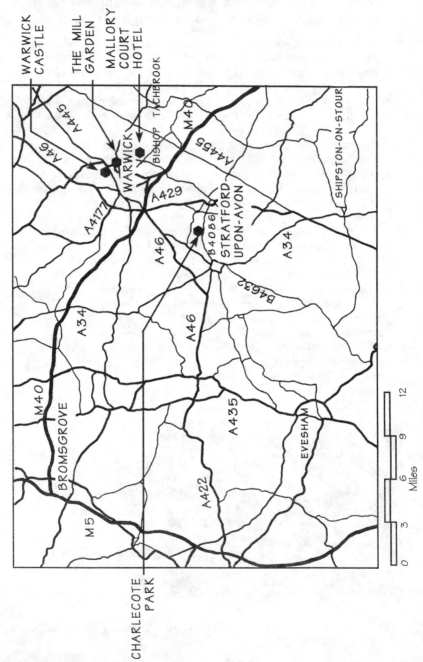

TOUR #18

* THE MILL GARDEN
* WARWICK CASTLE
* CHARLECOTE PARK

• FRIDAY THROUGH TUESDAY •

A quiet place to stop before the excitement and pageantry of
Warwick Castle, that's the lovely little house and informal garden
at Mill Street. Look up and you will see that big old castle. Thirty
minutes to an hour will allow you time to enjoy. Warwick Castle,
I've said it before, this is an event!. Plan on three to four hours
here. Tea in the orangery at Charlecote Park sounds like a good
idea to me. There's also a great house, wonderful grounds and
lots of deer. A good place for a couple hours at the end of the day.
Travel time from The Mill Garden to Warwick Castle is about five
minutes. Travel time from Warwick Castle to Charlecote Park is
10 minutes.

THE MILL GARDEN
- Hours of Admission: 9:00 to dusk
- Location: beside Warwick Castle, 55 Mill St. (at the end)

  - What a contrast, standing in this lovely, little perennial garden and
    looking up at that big old castle.
  - Enjoy this cute little house and series of informal garden areas on the
    river beneath Warwick
    Castle.
  - You will find the remains of a
    great old vine covered bridge
    that once connected to the
    castle to the far side of the
    river.
  - The mood is quiet with
    wonderful water sounds. A
    good way to start the day
    and your visit to Warwick.

Warwick Castle
looms above the
cottage garden at
Mill Street.

WARWICK CASTLE

- Hours of Admission: 10:00 to 6:00
- Location: 8 miles northeast of Stratford-on-Avon

  - This is an event! Visit for many reasons including the gardens.
  - You will find a mediaeval castle with ancient and chivalrous splendor.
  - It was originally built by William the Conqueror in 1066 and played a prominent part in English history for 700 years.
  - There are 60 acres of grounds and gardens that were landscaped by "Capability" Brown. By the end of the 18th century the gardens had been planted and the castle was basically as we see it today.
  - The Victorian rose garden created in 1868 was restored to its original beauty in 1986. It is very formal in design using all old fashion roses.
  - Look for the Peacock Garden, a quiet formal garden in front of Conservatory.
  - The Pageant Field is a parkland skirted by many fine trees some as old as 200 years.
  - Note: This is a popular spot and there are always a lot of people. Admission is a little steep (£8.75) but what an experience!

Walk into the fairy tale world of Warwick Castle.

NOTE: Mallory Court Hotel, wonderful place to stay while your touring the area or just a place to visit for its lovely gardens. A charming country hotel with a Michelin-rated restaurant. Located at Bishops Tachbrook, Leamington Spa phone (01926) 330214

NOTE: St. Nicholis Park in Warwick is lovely. You might want to stop by for a few minutes while you are in town.

The refurbished walls and knot garden at Charlecote Park.

CHARLECOTE PARK (N.T.)
- Hours of Admission: 11:00 to 6:00
- Location: 4 miles east of Stratford-on-Avon on B4086

  - Home of the Lucy family since 1247 and given to National Trust in 1946 along with 180 acres of fenced deer park.
  - The house dates from the mid 16th century, but was substantially remodeled in the Elizabethan Revival style in early 19th century. Enjoy all the fru-fru, steeples and stained glass.
  - Many of the lovely formal features of the original garden were swept away for the natural look by "Capability" Brown.
  - One of the 16th Century features that still remains is a formal garden, with clipped yews, terraces and urns planted with geraniums & lobelia.
  - It is said that William Shakespeare poached deer here. To "commemorate" the occasions a border has been planted with species mentioned in his plays (columbine, dog violets).
  - This is a good example of the care the National Trust takes in refurbishing. The cut out stone walls off the back of the house had deteriorated so badly they had to be replaced. Pictures were used to duplicate the original design in the new stone work, a fantastic job.
  - In addition, the knot garden was replanted in its original location. Again an old picture was used to duplicate the original design.
  - Approximately 250 Fallow deer roam freely in a preserve seen from the garden. There are black Roman, spotted Menil and 150 Red deer.
  - The 19th century orangery is a lovely place for tea or lunch.

OTHER GARDENS IN THE AREA: BADDESLEY CLINTON, PACKWOOD HOUSE

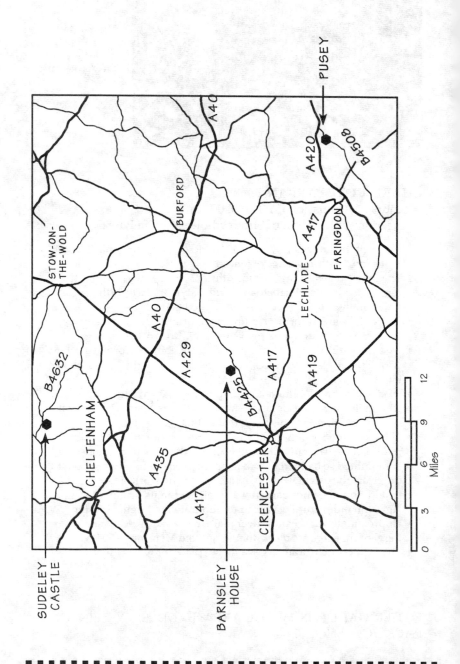

TOUR # 19

* **BARNSLEY HOUSE**
* **SUDELEY CASTLE**
* **PUSEY**

• TUESDAY, WEDNESDAY, THURSDAY •

This tour covers a broad area of the Cotswolds. Enjoy the scenery as well as the gardens. A visit to Barnsley House is a visit to one of Britain's best known gardens. There are many garden styles and a rainbow of colors to enjoy. A minimum of two hours is needed here. Sudeley Castle is romance, history and charming gardens. A truly wonderful garden, Pusey is a private home known for its borders. The main border is 150 yards long with hundreds of perennials, roses and peonies. Plan on one to two hours each for Sudeley Castle and Pusey. Travel time from Barnsley House to Sudeley is 1 hour. Travel time from Sudeley to Pusey is 1 hour & 15 minutes.

BARNSLEY HOUSE

- Hours of Admission: 10:00 to 6:00
- Location: 4 miles northeast of Cirencester on B4425

  - One of the best known gardens in Britain and created by one of England's best loved gardeners, Rosemary Verey.
  - You will see a 17th century gabled house that was previously a rectory, a stone wall that was built in 1771 and perimeter trees that were planted in 1840. Work on the four acre garden you see today did not begin until the early 1960's.
  - Mrs. Verey is a great experimenter and each part of garden has its own character. She has used her knowledge of garden history to plan and plant many areas of the garden in historical styles.
  - The many garden styles are blended well. There is the very formal knot garden, planted in 1975, and in contrast, there is the "wilderness" area planted with ornate trees.
  - Look for the much photographed laburnum tunnel, it is truly wonderful, especially in early June.
  - Borders are a collection of plants selected for their shape, color, scent and year-round interest.
  - You will find an eighteen century Tuscan temple with a goldfish pond, the feeling is very peaceful.
  - Intricate potager beds mix roses and clematis with fruits and vegetables.
  - Interesting old sculptures by Simon Verity, such as "Lady with Basket" and "Victorian Woman", are scattered throughout.
  - This is the kind of garden that all of us serious gardeners would like to create and enjoy.

Shapes and shapes of topiaries at Sudeley Castle.

SUDELEY CASTLE

- Hours of admission: 10:30 to 5:30
- Location: 6 miles northeast of Cheltenham on A46, turn east at Winchcombe
  - This was the home of Queen Katherine Parr (Henry VIII's 6th wife) in the 16th century.
  - The castle is still standing but several other buildings were partially destroyed by Cromwell's troops during the Reformation.
  - Look for the lovely rectangular lily pond that sits in front of the magnificent tithe barn ruins.
  - The walls of these same ruins provide a great backdrop for a wonderful walled garden with roses climbing everywhere.
  - An award winning Tudor rose garden, the Queen's Garden, was laid out by Emma Dent in the mid 19th century and is an imitation of the medieval original. There are hundreds of varieties of old fashioned English roses.
  - The Knot Garden was opened to commemorate the anniversary of Queen Elizabeth I's visit to the castle in 1592. The design was inspired by dress fabric worn by the Queen in a painting hanging in the castle.
  - You will find a number of wonderful hedges that seem to require extensive and continual trimming.
  - Note: The gardens are not spectacular but pretty, charming and very romantic, what a movie set!

The brilliant gold of the laburnum attracts many photographers to this tunnel at Barnsley House.

PUSEY

- Hours of Admission: 2:00 to 6:00
- Location: 10 miles southwest of Oxford on A420
  turn south onto B4508

  - A charming garden with Cotswold stone walls, big old trees, and exceptional herbaceous borders. The main border is 150 yards long and considered one of the most impressive in England (primary color is blue).
  - The stone house was built in 1748 but the gardens were created much more recently by Geoffrey Jellicoe who began refurbishing and creating the grounds in 1937.
  - You enter through a side gate and are greeted by two colorful borders. You continue on and pass through the iron gate at the end of the path and discover a full panoramic view of the garden.
  - A unique Oriental inspired bridge built in 1755 crosses a lovely lake with swans, ducks, fish and water lilies. The bridge has strong horizontal lines, diagonal bracing and crisp white paint.
  - From the lake you look back to spreading lawn leading up to the manor house and lovely terraced beds filled with flowers and many shrub roses.
  - Lady Emily's Garden is a small secluded garden planted mainly with roses. Clematis, hydrangeas and roses cover the brick walls.
  - A private home with a truly wonderful garden.

A view of the 16th century manor house from the lake at Pusey.

OTHER GARDENS IN THE AREA: BUSCOT PARK, MISARDEN PARK

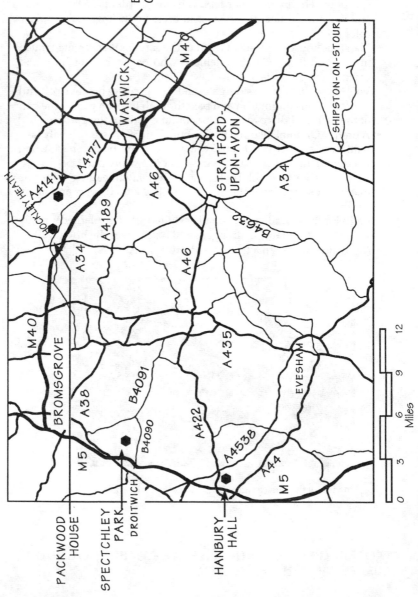

TOUR # 20

* SPECTCHLEY PARK
* BADDESLEY CLINTON
* PACKWOOD HOUSE

• WEDNESDAY AND SUNDAY •

Owned by the Berkeley family (Berkeley Castle), the design and plant materials at Spetchley are terrific. Plan on approximately an hour here. Now take a scenic drive through the English countryside until you reach Baddesley Clinton. This is a wonderful Norman looking castle with a moat and lovely grounds. I fell in love with this small castle. Your next stop is one of my absolute favorites. Packwood House is glorious with its colorful borders, lovely walled gardens and famous clipped yews. You will need a little over an hour at Baddesley Clinton and a minimum of two hours at Packwood House. Travel time from Spetchley to Baddesley Clinton is 1 hour. Travel time from Baddesley Clinton to Packwood House is 10 minutes.

SPETCHLEY PARK
- Hours of Admission: 11:00 to 5:00
- Location: 3 miles east of Worcester on A423

  - Rowland Berkeley, a direct descendant of the Lords of Berkeley of Berkeley Castle, purchased the estate in 1605.
  - The original house, a moated Tudor, was burned down in 1651 by a band of disgruntled Scots. The present Georgian manor was built in 1811.
  - Little change has taken place in the parkland since the 17th century but, unfortunately, the avenues of elms had to be cut down in the 1970's because of Dutch elm disease.
  - The 30 acre garden has experienced many changes over the years as each generation has added their own touch. Much of the current garden was designed by Ellen Willmott.
  - You will find lovely borders, 36 yew hedged garden beds, a kitchen garden, a rose lawn with conservatory, great old trees and a wonderful lake.
  - Note: This is a place to be admired. The overall design and plant materials are wonderful but the maintenance is not up to the highest standards.

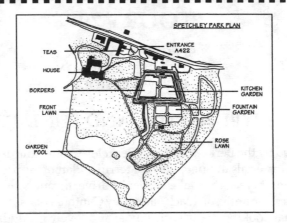

BADDESLEY CLINTON (N.T.)

- Hours of Admission: 2:00 to 6:00
- Location: 7.5 miles north of Warwick on A4141

  - The history of the property dates back to the 13th century when the Clintons settled and dug the moat. Most of the house, however, is no earlier than the 15th century.
  - The home of a lesser English gentry, it lacks the ostentation of the huge estates. The house is unique in its simplicity with a brick bridge entrance over the moat, a gatehouse with gun ports and a facade that has been updated several times over the centuries.
  - Lands of smaller gentry were frequently bought up by larger estates so it is rare to find the lands of this estate much as it was described in a survey map of 1699.
  - The property was sold several times. The last time was in 1438 to John Brome. His granddaughter married Sir Edward Ferrers whose family held Baddesley until 1939.
  - You will note that the forecourt and lovely walled garden remain from early 18th century.
  - The Victorian period provided the wooded setting with big, purple rhododendrons.
  - Enjoy a peaceful walk around the chain of 15th century fish ponds with swans and water plants.
  - The National Trust acquired the property in 1980.
  - Note-Take in the whole experience, the natural looking landscape and the marvelous Norman looking castle. It's very simple and very impressive. Well worth the trip.

The gate house at Baddesley Clinton.

PACKWOOD HOUSE (N.T.)

- Hours of Admission: 2:00 to 6:00
- Location: 11 miles southeast of central Birmingham on A34 turn east onto B4439 at Hockley Heath

- You will find seven glorious acres of topiaries, borders, walled gardens and some wonderful and unusual details.
- The main block of the house was built in the late 16th Century by the Fetherston family who lived there for nearly 300 years.
- Rising out of the lawn is a remarkable perennial garden with colorful borders and yew hedges surrounding a lovely sunken pool.
- One of the more unusual details is in the rose garden. The bed is backed by a brick wall but the varieties are separated by yew walls.
- Enjoy the elevated double herbaceous border which leads the way from one elevated brick garden house to the other. This section is just gorgeous, very different and provides a glorious view of the garden.
- The austere beauty of the famous yew garden provides an interesting contrast. It was originally set out by John Fetherston c. 1650-1670 is said to represent "The Sermon on the Mount".
- Many of the pieces of furniture found in the house where purchased in the 1930's by Baron Ash from nearby Baddesley Clinton. This saved much of the collection. You will also find a wonderful collection of tapestries.
- Mr. Graham Baron Ash, who had spent time and money restoring the house to its original form, gave a total of 113 acres to the National Trust in 1941.
- Note: One of my absolute favorites!

Unusual treatment of boxwood hedges and roses at Packwood House.

Note: Hanbury Hall, a lovely National Trust garden, is on the way to Baddesley Clinton. Unfortunately it does not open until 2:00 and I was concerned that three gardens in one afternoon would be too much. It is indicated on the map if you want to visit this one as well. See "Garden Descriptions on page 104 for further information.

OTHER GARDENS IN THE AREA: CHARLECOTE PARK, MILL GARDEN, WARWICK CASTLE

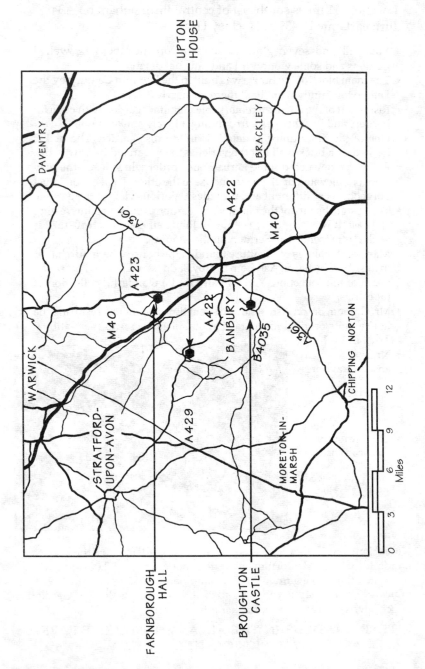

TOUR # 21

* UPTON HOUSE
* BROUGHTON CASTLE
* FARNBOROUGH HALL

• WEDNESDAY •

This will be a busy Wednesday afternoon but you can do it. The terraced gardens and bog area at Upton House are some of the best I've ever seen. This place will really surprise you. Expect to climb lots of steps and spend up to two hours. A moated castle in the middle of beautiful English countryside, that's what you will find at Broughton Castle. At Farnborough Hall you will find lovely grounds, charming people and a quaint little rose garden. Expect to do a lot of walking if you want to see it all. At least an hour is right for your visit to Broughton and Farnborough. Travel time from Upton House to Broughton Castle is 15 minutes. Travel time from Broughton Castle to Farnborough Hall is 15 minutes.

BROUGHTON CASTLE

- Hours of Admission: 2:00 to 5:00
- Location: 2.5 miles southwest of Banbury on B4035

  - A lovely moated castle built between 1300 and 1550 lies in the midst of a beautiful English pasture.
  - Owned by the same family for over 600 years, it is currently the home of Lord and Lady Saye and Sele.
  - Three acres of open grassy meadows, big old chestnut trees and wonderful borders.
  - A walled garden at the foot of the castle contains flower beds hedged by boxwoods and borders of perennials and shrub roses all in soft pinks, whites and purples. Quite a contrast to the 12th Century castle looming above.
  - One of the more beautiful places in England, especially in June & July.

Gateway to the wonders of Broughton Castle.

UPTON HOUSE (N.T.)

- Hours of Admission: 2:00 to 6:00
- Location: 7 miles northwest of Banbury on A422

  - Sir Rushout Cullen made a major contribution to the original layout of the garden in addition to building the central part of the house in 1695.
  - A major renovation of the house and garden began in 1927. Lord Bearsted worked with architect Morley Horder on the house and wide terraces behind the house and Lady Bearsted with guidance from Kitty Lloyd-Jones created one of Upton's greatest pleasures, its garden.
  - The upper terrace, at the house, is planted with lavender, catmint and old Scots rose "Williams Double Yellow".
  - You are in for quite a surprise here. Standing at the house you look out across a large lawn area which appears to merge with the pasture land in the distance. But step to the edge of the lawn, look down and you will discover an extraordinary terraced garden with brick stairs and big, old trees along the edges.
  - At the bottom is a lake with fountains of grasses and lovely water lilies. Stand at the lake and look back, the house is hidden but the view of the terraces is wonderful.
  - On the terraces you will find "Her Ladyship's Garden", a yew enclosed rose garden with a colorful assortment of flowers, the NCCPG National Collection of asters and fruits & vegetables laid out like a French potager on the warm south slope.
  - The Bog Garden, one of the biggest I've ever seen, is fabulous with its hostas, gunnera, rodgersias along with primulas, astilbes and irises that fill it with luxuriant foliage.
  - Look for the large, traditionally English kitchen garden, the sections of vegetables are divided by rows of fruit bushes.
  - The property was given to the National Trust in 1948.
  - Note: If you can, take the opportunity to visit the house. It contains one of the finest private art collections assembled in England this century.

The stairway that leads
you up from the lake
through the
extraordinary terraced
garden at Upton House.

FARNBOROUGH HALL (N.T.)

- Hours of Admission: 2:00 to 6:00
- Location: 6 miles north of Banbury, .5 miles west of A423

  - Purchased by Ambrose Holbech in 1684, Farnborough has been in the Holbech family ever since.
  - You will see wonderful views of the village and the countryside and sheep that are grazing everywhere.
  - An untouched 18th century elysium was devised by William Holbech with guidance from Sanderson Miller about 1745. Holbech made the grand tour of Europe and was greatly influenced by landscapes and gardens he had seen in France and Italy.
  - A three quarter of a mile Terrace Walk in an ascending, serpentine curve starting at house has panoramic views from the Ionic Temple and the Oval Temple.
  - Look for a lovely little rose garden hedged by yews and boxwood below the house.
  - A wonderful Obelisk was originally built before 1751 and rebuilt after it collapsed in 1823.
  - The 160 acre estate became part of the National Trust in 1960
  - Note: Take a little time to see the house. Mr. Geoffrey Holbech may greet you at the door. He is charming and very dignified and if he finds out you are from California, he will be pleased to tell you he has a son in San Diego. The Lady of the House may be sitting at the top of the beautiful staircase and she will be happy to tell you its story.

Rose garden and fountain at Farnborough Hall.

OTHER GARDENS IN THE AREA: BROOK COTTAGE

LOTS N' LOTS
OF
HELPFUL
INFORMATION

Barnsley House, Gloucestershire

• GARDEN DESCRIPTIONS •

1. BADDESLEY CLINTON (N.T.)
• 7.5 miles north of Warwick on A41

The history of this castle dates back to the 13th century. Most of the house, however, was built in the 15th century. The estate is unique in its simplicity and rare to find its lands intact, much as it was in 1699. It was purchased in 1438 by John Brome. His granddaughter married Sir Edward Ferrers whose family held Baddesley until 1939. The forecourt and lovely walled gardens remain from the 18th century. The Victorian Period provided the wooded setting with big, purple rhododendrons. See Tours 16 and 20.

2. BARNSLEY HOUSE
• 4 miles northeast of Cirencester on A433

One of the best known gardens in Britain. It was created by one of England's best loved gardeners, Rosemary Verey. The 17th century gabled house is surrounded by a two and a half acre garden that was begun in the early 1960's. The borders are a collection of plants selected for their shape, color, scent and year round interest. Mrs. Verey has blended many garden styles, including a formal knot garden, an intricate potager and a "wilderness" area. See Tours 4, 5 and 19.

3. BATSFORD PARK ARBORETUM
• 5 miles north of Stow-on-the-Wold on A429, turn west at Moreton-in-Marsh

The foundation was laid out by Lord Redesdale in the 1880's after he returned from a post as attaché in the British Embassy in Japan. It is distinctly Japanese in an English setting. This arboretum has an outstanding collection of plants including over 1500 named trees and shrubs. Interesting all year round but especially lovely in the spring with the flowering magnolias and cherries and in the fall with the color of maples, oaks and beeches. See Tour 12.

4. BERKELEY CASTLE
- at the town of Berkeley on B4066

A formidable castle and the home of the Berkeley family since the 12th century. This "Robin Hood" castle is the backdrop for a garden of simple terraces with grass walks and narrow, low growing borders. There is a wide selection of plants including roses, clematis, magnolias and a wisteria that rises the whole height of the castle. See Tours 2 and 3.

5. BLENHEIM PALACE
- 9 miles northwest of Oxford on A34

This wonderful estate was built by John Churchill, First Duke of Marborough, in 1705-1719 and is the birthplace of Winston Churchill. Several famous architects and designers had a hand in creating the garden and grounds you see today. Henry Wise and Achille Duchene provided the very formal areas such as the knot garden and Italian water garden with it's magnificent fountains. "Capability" Brown arrived in 1764 and created the two lakes and surrounding park. See Tours 6, 7 and 8.

6. BOURTON HOUSE GARDEN
- 2 miles west of Moreton-in-Marsh on A44

This is a formal three acre garden that has been reestablished over the last five years. The lush open lawn is broken up by fabulous planting beds that make the most of contrasts in foliage color, shape and size. One terrace has a nicely planted border and a lovely view of the countryside. This is a plantsmen's paradise. See Tours 12, 13 and 14.

7. BROOK COTTAGE
- 6 miles west of Banbury on A422, turn west toward Alkerton, turn opposite the war memorial

This is truly an English cottage garden, created by Mr. & Mrs. David Hodges over the last 30 years. You will find an unbelievable collection of over 300 roses and 50 different clematis. There is something to see in all seasons from bulbs and cherries in the spring to perennials and roses in the summer to autumn color in the fall. See Tour 15.

8. BROUGHTON CASTLE

- 2.5 miles southwest of Banbury on B4035

This lovely moated castle was built between 1300 and 1550 and lies in the middle of some of the most beautiful English pastureland. There are three acres of grassy meads, big old chestnuts and wonderful borders. A walled garden has borders of perennials and shrub roses, all in soft pinks, whites and purples. See Tour 15 and 21.

9. BUSCOT PARK (N.T.)

- 2.5 miles northwest of Faringdon on A417

This 18th century house is situated on a hill with glorious views in all directions. One of the vistas is provided by the Harold Peto water garden which carries the eye from the house, across the lake to a temple beyond. The Peter Coats border greats you as you enter the garden. It is an unusual border with plants selected to take advantage of contrasts in foliage color and shape. Classic brick walls set off the flower beds and climbing roses. See Tours 4 and 5.

10. CHARLECOTE PARK (N.T.)

- 4 miles east of Stratford-on-Avon on B4086

This magnificent house and formal garden date from the mid 16th century. The house, however, was substantially remodeled in the early 19th century in a more ornate style. Many of the lovely features of the original garden were swept away for the natural look by "Capability" Brown. But you will still find terraces displaying urns filled with colorful flowers, clipped yews, a rose garden and a knot garden that has recently been replanted in its original location. A deer preserve can be seen from the garden. It is said that William Shakespeare poached deer on this estate and one of the borders has been planted with species mentioned in his plays. See Tours 16 and 18.

11. FARNBOROUGH HALL (N.T.)

- 6 miles north of Banbury, 1/2 mile west of A423

The estate was purchased by Ambrose Holbech in 1684 and has been in the Holbech family since. William Holbech, who was greatly influenced by the gardens he had seen in his grand tour of France and Italy, designed the garden in 1745. There are lovely views of the countryside and sheep grazing everywhere. A three quarter of a mile Terrace Walk ascends from the house and provides wonderful views from the Ionic Temple and the Oval Temple. See Tour 21.

12. HANBURY HALL (N.T.)

- 4.5 miles east of Droitwich

A William and Mary style brick house from 1701. Although the large formal garden designed by George London was swept away in the late 18th century during the natural look movement, the National Trust began reconstruction of this formal garden in 1993. You will find a fine orangery built in 1735 and a replanted avenue leading to the well preserved 18th Century ice house which remain from London's design. See Tour 20.

13. HIDCOTE MANOR (N.T.)

- 3.5 miles north of Chipping Camden on B4081, turn east at junction with A46

One of the most famous gardens in Britain and one of the most influential English gardens of this century. It was created by an American, Lawrence Johnston, starting just prior to World War I. Designed like a house with rooms, there is a central hall or courtyard with rooms to the right and left. The structure is taken from the classical French but the planting is English with glorious colors. There are hedges of every description, a rose garden, a white garden and a pool garden with goldfish. Johnston personally collected many of the plants during his travels in Africa and China. See Tours 10 and 11.

14. HOW CAPLE COURT

- 10 miles south of Hereford on B4224; turn right at
  How Caple crossroads

An 11 acre Edwardian garden set high above the River Wye. The peaceful, rolling lawn has many large, mature trees and several specimen Japanese maples. Cotswold stone walls enclose the formal terraces planted with perennials and roses. The Florentine water garden is under restoration. See Tour 1.

15. HUNTS COURT

- 2 miles northwest of Wotton-under-Edge; from Wotton B4060 Dursley Rd turn right in Nibley at Black Horse Tavern

Created over the last 20 years by Keith & Margaret Marshall, this two and one half acre garden has over 30 varieties of hardy geraniums, 60 shrubby potentillas and a large collection of penstemons. But what people really come to see are the 400 varieties of roses. There are species, albas, damasks, gallicas, bourbons and many more. Most of which are never seen in the States. The trees and shrubs were planted to compliment the roses and provide a wonderful backdrop. See Tours 2 and 3.

16. KIFTSGATE COURT

- 3.5 miles north of Chipping Camden on B4081, turn east at junction with A46

The 19th century Georgian style house was built in 1887 but the garden was created after World War I by Mrs. Heather Muir. She had some help from her friend and neighbor, Major Johnston from Hidcote. Wide borders are planted in pinks, purples and crimson with gray foliage. There is a rose border, a yellow border and a white sunken garden. The views to the countryside are wonderful and feel like a part of the garden. The look is a little wild and cluttered but everything is in its proper place and a delight to behold. See Tour 10.

17. MALLORY COURT HOTEL

- Harbury Lane, Bishops Tachbrook, Leamington Spa

A charming country hotel with a Michelin-rated restaurant. Worth visiting for the garden alone but also a wonderful place to stay. See Tours 16, 17 and 18.

18. MILL GARDEN

- beside Warwick Castle, 55 Mill St. (at the end)

A cute little house and a series of informal areas on the river beneath Warwick Castle. The mood is quiet with wonderful water sounds. What a contrast, standing in this lovely perennial garden and looking up at such a formidable, old castle. See Tours 17 and 18.

19. MISARDEN PARK

- 6 miles northwest of Circencester follow the signs off the A417 or from Stroud take B4070

A beautiful 17th Century house stands overlooking Golden Valley and provides some great views. The house sits on a broad cut terrace and the terracing and sloping away of different gardens creates spectacular spaces and wonderful vistas. The walled garden with three border rows is one of the prettiest in England. See Tours 2 and 4.

20. OXFORD UNIVERSITY BOTANIC GARDEN

- in town center off High St., entrance opposite Magdalen College in Rose Lane

Founded in 1621, this is the oldest botanical garden in Britain and the second oldest in Europe. The flower beds are formal in their layout but informal in their planting. There is a demonstration garden of historical roses illustrating the origin of the garden rose. You will find several old trees such as a yew planted in 1650, a 120 year old magnolia and a Black pine planted in 1800. See Tours 6 and 8.

21. PACKWOOD HOUSE (N.T.)

- 11 miles southeast of central Birmingham on A34, turn east onto B4439 at Hockley Heath

The main block of the house was built in the late 16th century by the Fetherston family who lived there for nearly 300 years. The garden is 7 acres of topiaries, borders, walled gardens and some wonderful and unusual details. One feature, a sunken garden, rises out of the lawn and has perennial borders and yew hedges surrounding a lily pond. The most famous element is the yew garden originally set out around 1650-1670 and is said to represent "The Sermon on the Mount". See Tours 16, 17 and 20.

22. PAINSWICK ROCOCO GARDEN

• half mile outside village of Painswick on B4073

The manor was built in 1735 by Charles Hyett. His son Benjamin created the garden in the 1740's. This is the only complete survivor of the Rococo period. Restoration of the six acre garden began in 1984 and has stayed true to the original design. The Excedra Garden, a lovely perennial garden, was planted with over 20,000 18th century type plants. Several interesting structures are scattered about the property including the Red House, a Rococo style garden house. See Tour 1.

23. THE PRIORY

• in Kemerton, 5 miles northeast of Tewkesbury off B4080

This Georgian house and four acres were taken over by Mr. & Mrs. Peter Healing at the beginning of World War II. The original design for the garden was done on paper while Mr. Healing was serving with the RAF. Three lovely mixed borders include one almost completely red, one multi-colored and the third, the largest, has a range of colors from cool to warm. Look for the huge yew tree that dates from the 17th century and is clipped into a giant bun. See Tour 14.

24. PUSEY

• 10 miles southwest of Oxford on A420 turn south onto B4508

The stone house was built in 1748 but the gardens were created much more recently by Geoffrey Jellicoe starting in 1937. This is a private home with a truly wonderful garden filled with Cotswold stone walls, big old trees and exceptional herbaceous borders. A unique Oriental inspired bridge built in 1755 crosses the lake filled with swans, ducks, fish and waterlilies. From the lake you look back to a spreading lawn leading to the manor house and lovely terraced gardens. See Tour 5 and 19.

25. ROUSHAM PARK

- 14 miles north of Oxford on A423 turn east

A perfect example of the English landscape parks of the early 18th century. Created by William Kent from 1737 to 1741, it remains almost as it was and is one of the few gardens of this date to have escaped alteration. You will find a series of lovely walled gardens defined by either brick walls, trees or shrubs and containing colorful perennials, peonies and roses. In addition to the manor house, there is a small church that was built in 1214. See Tour 7.

26. SEZINCOTE

- 2 miles west of Moreton-in-Marsh on A44 turn south

Xanadu in England; the house is a Hindu-Mongul fantasy with its amber walls, copper dome and curving orangery. The house was completed in 1805 by Samual Pepys Cockerell for his brother Charles, who had served in the East India Co. Completed by 1810, the grounds are more like a park with many mature trees including magnificent cedars of Lebanon. The south garden is laid out in Mongul fashion with canals and paths crossing at right angles representing the rivers of life. See Tours 12 and 13.

27. SNOWSHILL MANOR (N.T.)

- 3 miles south of Broadway on road to Snowshill

Arts and Crafts Movement architect Charles Wade restored this old farm about 1920. The garden is organized in a series of terraces and outdoor rooms and the style of planting is colorful but unsophisticated with borders of mixed flowers and espalier trees. Sounds are an important part of the experience with a striking clock, Chinese wind chimes and many lovely water features. All doors, windows and gates are painted deep turquoise blue, now called Wade blue. See Tours 11 and 14.

28. SPETCHLEY PARK
- 3 miles east of Worcester on A423

Rowland Berkeley, a direct descendant of the Lords of Berkeley of Berkeley Castle, purchased the estate in 1605. The 30 acre garden has experienced many changes over the years as each generation has added its own touch. Much of the current garden was designed by Ellen Willmott. The overall design and plant materials are wonderful with colorful borders, a kitchen garden, the rose lawn with a conservatory, great old trees and a lovely lake. See Tour 20.

29. STOWE LANDSCAPE GARDENS (N.T.)
- 3 miles northwest of Buckingham off A422

May be the most important landscape gardens in Britain. Initially formal in design, the garden was started in the 16th century by Sir Richard Temple who spent 40 years and a great deal of money creating his dream. In the 18th century the Temple family employed many leading architects, landscape architects and sculptors including Vanbrugh, Bridgeman, Kent and Brown who created a landscape in the new naturalistic style of the period. There are 30 garden buildings and follies including temples, obelisks and a grotto. The National Trust acquired the property in 1989 and has embarked on one of the most ambitious and expensive programs of garden restoration ever undertaken in Britain. See Tour 9.

30. SUDELEY CASTLE
- 6 miles northeast of Cheltenham on A46, turn east at Winchcombe

The home of Queen Katherine Parr (Henry VIII's 6th wife) in the 16th century. Most of this charming castle is still standing but several other buildings were partially destroyed by Cromwell's troops during the Reformation. The walls of the ruins provide a great backdrop for a lovely walled garden, climbing roses and a formal lily pond. The Queen's Garden, an award winning Tudor rose garden, was laid out by Emma Dent in the mid 19th century and is an imitation of the medieval original. The Knot Garden was opened to commemorate the anniversary of Queen Elizabeth I's visit in 1592 and was inspired by dress fabric worn by the Queen in a painting hanging in the castle. See Tours 10, 11, 13 and 19.

31. UPTON HOUSE (N.T.)

- 7 miles northwest of Banbury on A422

The central part of the house was built in 1695 by Sir Rushout Cullen. He also made a considerable contribution to the layout of the garden. From the house you look out across a large lawn area which appears to merge with the pastureland in the distance. As you approach the edge, you look down and discover a beautiful terraced garden with big, old trees along the edges. At the bottom is a lake with grasses and gold fish. If you turn and look back, the view of the terraces is spectacular. A large bog garden contains some fantastic plants such as hostas, gunnera, rodgersias, primulas, astilbes and irises. See Tour 15 and 21.

32. WADDESDON MANOR (N.T.)

- 6 miles northwest of Aylesbury on A41

Baron Ferdinand de Rothschield began construction of the house and reshaping of the grounds in 1874. In 1989 the partnership of the Rothschield family and the National Trust undertook a major restoration and determined that the grounds be returned, as nearly as possible, to their original state. Beth Rothschield designed the new parterre with the intent to restore the effect of the turn-of-the-century bedding. A total of 25,000 plants were used in 1993. The 18th century Italian and Dutch garden sculptures collected by Baron Ferdinand still occupy their original positions and are unrivaled as a collection in Britain. See Tours 8 and 9.

33. WARWICK CASTLE

- 8 miles northeast of Stratford-on-Avon

This mediaeval castle was originally built by William the Conqueror in 1066 and it has played a prominent part in English history for 700 years. The 60 acres of grounds and gardens were created by "Capability" Brown. The Victorian rose garden was created in 1868 and restored in 1986. Its design is very formal and the roses are all of the old fashion type. By the end of the 18th century the gardens had been planted and the castle was essentially as we see it today. An event to be experienced! See Tours 17 and 18.

34. WATERPERRY HORTICULTURAL CENTER

- 6 miles east of Oxford on A40; turn northeast at Holton to Waterperry

Founded in the 1930's as a horticultural college for young ladies There are 83 acres of walled gardens that now contain a nursery and garden center. Open grassy areas weave through planting beds and almost 100 yards of magnificent herbaceous perennial borders backed by brick walls. There is a wonderful alpine garden and a rock garden full of colorful perennials. See Tours 6, 7, 8 and 9.

35. WESTBURY COURT GARDEN (N.T.)

- 9 miles southwest of Gloucester on A48

One of the rarest types of gardens to survive in Britain, a formal late 17th century water garden influenced by Dutch ideas. Laid out by Maynard Colchester, digging of the Long Canal was begun in 1696. The T-Canal and Gazebo were probably built around 1715 by Colchester's nephew, Maynard Colchester II. A spectacular Neptune fountain stands at the end of the T-Canal. Recently replanted and restored, the old Dutch style has been closely adhered to. A small Walled Garden is planted with almost 100 species of plants, types that were grown in England before 1700. In addition, 40 kinds of old roses from the same period were planted. See Tour 1.

36. WESTONBIRT ARBORETUM

- 3.5 miles southwest of Tetbury on A433

This is an arboretum and park with lovely specimen trees that was begun in 1829 by Robert Holford. Many new conifers were imported from North America such as Douglas fir, noble fir, coast redwood and sequoia. There is a wonderful collection of ornamental cherries and maples. The rhododendrons, azaleas and bluebells make a glorious spring. Great fall color comes from the many large trees. See Tour 3.

• BIOGRAPHIES OF GARDENERS •

Charles Bridgeman (d. 1738)

Most notable works: Chiswick House, London; Claremont, Surrey; Kensington Gardens, London; Rousham House, Oxfordshire; Stowe, Buckinghamshire

- He helped bridge the gap between the formality of the late 17th century and the emerging "landscape" period.
- His style retained the details and characteristics of formality but was asymmetrical and presented a relationship between the garden and the surrounding countryside.
- A practical gardening knowledge and his professional training as a surveyor which enabled him to cope with large scale designs were his two main assets. He could convert ideas onto paper and then into reality.
- He was a pupil of George London & Henry Wise, the leading gardening partnership during the reign of William & Mary.
- In 1728 he succeeded Wise as the royal gardener and retained that position until his death.
- Much of his work was altered or destroyed by "Capability" Brown and others during the "Landscape Movement".
- He worked on Stowe & Claremont with Sir John Vanbrugh and was greatly influenced by his style. Bridgeman continued to work at Stowe from 1715 until shortly before his death in 1738.
- Although Rousham Park is acknowledged as William Kent's most outstanding work, he did work closely within the framework of Bridgeman's original layout. Some of Bridgeman's features still remain such as the "natural theater" and the bowling green lawn.
- He is considered by many to be the first to use the "ha-ha" in England.

Lancelot "Capability" Brown- 1716-1783

Most notable works: too numerous to list them all but those included in this book are Blenheim Palace, Oxfordshire; Charlecote Park, Warwickshire; Stowe, Buckinghamshire; Warwick Castle, Warwickshire

- Even after 200 years, Brown's stamp on the English countryside remains unmistakable. His work was so close to nature that, since the landscapes have now reached maturity, it is indistinguishable.

Brown (continued)

- He did destroy many lovely gardens but he did create many fine landscapes and established a garden style that belonged to Britain alone.
- During his 40 year career he refined the concept of landscape so that it became dependent on three simple factors: trees, water, terrain.
- His ideal landscape had gentle contours, water and a minimum of man-made interruptions. To achieve his goal he planted thousands of native trees, moved huge qualities of earth and damned streams to create lakes.
- Brown took the job as head gardener at Stowe when he was in his twenties. He learned from the work of William Kent and eventually contributed to the last two major phases of Stowe's development.
- By the time Brown left Stowe (after 9 years), he had already completed several commissions and had established himself as the leading landscape designer of the day.
- In his redesign of Warwick Castle, he removed the small formal gardens and replaced them with lawn.
- He was appointed surveyor to His Majesty's gardens and waters at Hampton Court in 1764.

Peter Coats (20th Century)
Most notable garden works: Buscot Park, Oxfordshire

- A well known writter on horticultural sujects and author of *Great Gardens of Britain, Great Gardens of the Western World* and *The House & Garden Book of Beautiful Gardens*.
- A long time gardening editor of House & Garden magazine.
- A practicing garden designer, he created the Peter Coats Border at Buscot Park.

Achille Duchene (1866-1947)
Most notable works: Blenheim Palace, Oxfordshire

- His style reflected the "golden age" of French gardening and he was one of the first garden designers to enjoy an international career.
- Blenheim was his only British commission. He was hired to restore it to its 18th century glory.

- On the east side of the palace he laid out the formal parterre around a circular pool that was reminiscent of Henry Wise's early 18th century work at Blenheim.
- In addition, after World War I, he created the water terraces to the west between the palace and "Capability" Brown's lake.

Robert Holford (1808-1892)

Most notable works: Westonbirt, Gloucestershire
- Although Holford inherited the Westonbirt estate and the fortune to finance his work in 1839, he really begun work on the arboretum 10 years earlier.
- He planted a range of trees that allowed him to combine botanical interest with the pleasure of arrangement and grouping.
- For the last 20 years of his life Holford worked at Westonbirt in partnership with his son George.

Sir Geoffrey Jellicoe (1900- 1996)

Most notable works: Ditchley Park, Oxfordshire; Royal Lodge, Berkshire; Sutton Place, Surrey; Pusey, Oxfordshire
- He is generally acknowledged as one of the foremost British garden and landscape designer of the 20th century.
- He had the ability to reconcile the traditions of the past with contemporary ideas. In his early years he combined his admiration for Italian Renaissance gardens with a strong commitment to modernism as demonstrated at Ditchley Park.

Gertrude Jekyll (1843-1932)

Most notable works: too numerous to list but a few examples are Barrington Court, Somerset; Hestercombe, Somerset; Lambay Castle, Eire; Marsh Court, Hampshire; Munstead Wood, Surry; Woodside, Buckinghamshire

- Jekyll made an unequaled contribution to the foundation of gardens as we know them today. She demonstrated how gardening could best be scaled down in a modest home without sacrificing on quality or interest.
- She helped to bridge the gap between professional and amateur gardeners and promoted the involvement of women.

Jekyll (continued)

- A simple portrait of Jekyll indicates she was trained as a painter and worked as a craftswoman. She had an encyclopedic memory of both wild and cultivated plants and a fondness for the simple life.
- Preferring the small and intimate to the large and expansive, she paid attention to detail in plant color, in form and in architectural materials.
- A friendship and working relationship developed between Jekyll and Edwin Lutyens. The most fruitful years of their partnership were 1897 to 1908.
- Certain guidelines and techniques were constants in all Jekyll and Lutyen's work together: 1) unity between house and garden, 2) between planting and architectural features, 3) between various areas of the garden.
- Unfortunately, little of her work remains in its original form.
- She began her writing career in the 1870's with magazine articles in *The Garden* and she wrote her first book in 1899.

Major Lawrence Johnston (1871-1958)

Most notable work: Hidcote Manor, Gloucestershire

- Johnston was an American, who was born in Paris, educated in England and became a naturalized British citizen in 1900.
- The farm at Hidcote was purchased for him by his mother on his return from the war in South Africa.
- He had no practical experience or professional training but he did have a clear idea of how the garden should evolve.
- Johnston was able to indulge his acquired skills and knowledge of plants in all the different planting beds he created. He enclosed those beds with a variety of hedges including hollies, yews, beeches and hornbeams.
- He joined two plant collecting expeditions between 1907 and 1914, the first to southern Africa, the second to Yunnan in China.

William Kent (1685-1748)

Most notable works: Chiswick House, London; Claremont, Surrey; Rousham House, Oxfordshire; Stowe, Buckinghamshire

- He initiated the change known as the "landscape movement" at the beginning of the 18th century.

- Horace Walpole called him "The father of modern gardening. He leapt the fence and saw that all nature was a garden." The influence of Kent's garden designs was enormous through the balance of the 18th century and beyond.
- Although we consider him a painter, landscape gardener and architect, he was more architect as seen from the structures (temples, obelisks, gateways) he put into his plans.
- He had a more visual approach to design. There is no evidence that he drew up plans or wrote down his ideas (except in letters) which allowed him to create with a greater freshness.
- Kent spent nine years in Italy starting in his late twenties. The architecture, paintings and gardens he studied there were a great inspiration to him throughout his career.
- Probably the most significant influence to his career as a landscape architect was Alexander Pope who believed that "all gardening is landscape painting".
- He added his own ideas to the designs of Bridgeman at Stowe, Rousham and Claremont. Rousham is considered Kent's masterpiece.

George London (d. 1713)

Most notable works: Blenheim Palace, Oxfordshire; Hampton Court, London; Melbourne Hall, Derbyshire; Hanbury Hall, Hereford & Worcester

- In 1681 London established Brompton Nurseries, the first English commercial nursery. He was joined by Henry Wise in 1687.
- The partnership of London & Wise was the foremost designer of formal gardens during the reigns of William & Mary and Queen Anne.
- Influences from Italy and France were incorporated into the English landscape.
- The formality of the hedges and the intricate patterns of gardens beds they created at places like Blenheim Palace caused some of the strongest reactions from members of the landscape movement.
- Unfortunately much of their work disappeared in the face of that more naturalistic style of the 18th century.

Sir Edwin Lutyens (1869-1944)

Most notable works: too numerous to provide a total list but a few examples are Eaton Hall, Cheshire; Great Dexter, Sussex; Long Barn, Kent

- One of the most original and sought-after architects of his time.
- He met Gertrude Jekyll when he was just 20 and his education as an architect was influenced in such a manner to set him apart from his contemporaries.
- His partnership with Jekyll created a wonderful harmony between house and garden, a place to live in, a place to enjoy. The balance they sought formed a cornerstone for 20th century gardens.
- In later years Lutyens developed a more individual and classical style demonstrated in the grand formal canal gardens he created after World War I.
- His garden architecture stressed the importance of strong directional lines and horizontal and vertical surfaces again demonstrated in his strong hedges.
- He created some of the best known garden furniture designs of the early 20th century.

William Morris (1834-1896)

- Morris was a designer and decorator, a creator of wonderful textiles, a poet and political activist and the "creator" of the Arts & Crafts Movement of the 19th Century.
- He rebelled against the Victorian period and his own privileged upbringing and grew to believe in the simplicities of life.
- His concept of the ideal home was: "Have nothing in your houses that you do not know to be useful, or believe to be beautiful."
- In 1861 he set up the Morris & Co. firm, a decorating company that provided not only decorating services but products such as fabrics and wallpapers.

Harold Peto (1854-1933)

Most notable works: Buscot Park, Oxfordshire; Heale House, Wiltshire; Wayford Manor, Somerset

- Peto had an architects eye and a true feel for the use of plants.
- He had a great admiration for the delights of Renaissance Italy and a growing interest in the relationship between house and garden.

- In 1876 he established an architectural partnership with Ernest George. It became one of the most respected practices of the late Victorian and Edwardian periods.
- In 1886 Edwin Lutyens was taken on as a pupil.
- Peto set up his own firm in 1892 and offered garden design and garden architecture.
- At Buscot Park he designed the wonderful hedge-lined water garden that drops down to the lake. This is his most masterly design and in the true Renaissance tradition.

Alexander Pope (1688-1744)

- Pope, who believed that "all gardening is landscape painting", was the most significant influence to Charles Kent's career as a landscape architect.
- He was a successful writer, a political essayist and an influential figure of the day.
- His influence on artistic taste was probably greater than that of any of his contemporaries.
- He not only had a visual image of the classical garden in harmony with the surrounding English countryside but also an interest in the practical side of horticulture.

Humphry Repton (1752-1818)

Most notable works: too numerous to list but a few examples are Sezincote, Gloucestershire; Longnor Hall, Shropshire; Sarsden House, Oxfordshire

- "Capability" Brown's successor, he adapted the "landscape movement" to the emerging prosperous middle class. He added "practicality" to Kent and Brown's ideas.
- In 1788, in his late 30's, with little formal training, he turned from architecture to garden design out of financial necessity. In a very short time he had a busy and successful career with recommendations from many satisfied clients.
- For Repton four requisites were needed for a perfect landscape design: 1)design must hide natural defects and display natural beauties, 2)boundaries should be carefully hidden or disguised, 3)the look should be natural, 4)objects of convenience or comfort must be removed or concealed if it isn't possible to make them part of the general scenery.
- He sited houses near the buildings (barns, stables, etc.) that serviced the household and he felt that the style of the house should be closely reflected in the style of its surroundings.

Repton (continued)

- He had a feeling for the use of plants and a knowledge of their appropriateness to compliment various architectural styles.
- He reintroduced the terrace and, to a certain extent, flowers to the garden.
- A "Red Book" system for presenting proposals to each client was created.
- Like so many others, much of his work has either disappeared or been seriously altered.

Sir John Vanbrugh (1664-1726)

Most notable works: Queen's Theatre, London; Blenheim Palace, Oxfordshire; Claremont, Surrey; Stowe, Buckinghamshire
- Vanbrugh was a soldier, a playwrite and, finally, an architect.
- He developed a style of baroque architecture that was unique in England.
- The idea that gardens, like painted landscapes, are composed of lakes, temples, woods and vistas was first conceived by Vanbrugh.
- He was committed to a strongly structured, balanced, geometric plan.
- He worked with Charles Bridgeman on Claremont and Stowe. Unfortunately, out of all the garden buildings he designed at Stowe only the rotunda still survives.

Rosemary Verey (1918-)

Most notable works: Barnsley House, Gloucestershire; Highgrove House, Gloucestershire; Little House, Gloucestershire
- One of the best known contemporary garden authorities in England. Mrs. Verey exemplifies the manor in which "amateur" gardeners and garden writers have influenced today's garden.
- The foundations of her garden work are a fascination with garden history and a love of plants.
- She has had great success incorporating period features from Tudor and 17th century gardens into a modern design.
- Since 1980 she has written several books on garden design and style.
- Barnsley House, her best known work and her home, has provided much of the research and material for her books.

- She has also designed borders, knot gardens and formal kitchen gardens for places like The Old Rectory, Ascot Place, Mount Stuart and Sudeley Castle. In each case, the new additions have fitted harmoniously into the existing garden.

Charles Wade (1883-1956)

Most notable work: Snowshill Manor, Gloucestershire

- A scholar, architect and artist craftsman, Wade purchased Snowshill in 1919.
- He believed that the plan of a garden is more important than the flowers and that the visitor should be lured into exploring beyond what is immediate, that mystery is important in the design.
- After he restored the old farm, he lived there in rather spartan conditions (he never had electric lights) and spent his time and fortune accumulating an incredible collection of objects.

Horace Walpole (1717-1797)

- A novelist, political essayist and commentator of the times whose Gothic essay, Strawberry Hill, is recognized as the main impetus for the Gothic revival in Britain.
- He held gardening talents in high esteem and he wrote the "History of the Modern Taste in Gardening".

Henry Wise (1653-1738)

Most notable works: Blenheim Palace, Oxfordshire; Hampton Court, London; Melbourne Hall, Derbyshire

- In 1687 Wise joined George London at Brompton Nurseries, the first English commercial nursery. It was the principal source of plants and trees in England.
- The partnership of London & Wise continued until 1713 and was the foremost designer of formal gardens during the reigns of William & Mary and Queen Anne.
- The royal gardener to Queen Anne, he was commissioned to work on Blenheim Palace with Sir John Vanbrugh.

• GARDEN DESIGN PERIODS •

FORMAL GARDEN DESIGN

In the 16th Century the pleasure garden began to appear. Instead of being a place to just look at, it became a place to spend time in, to entertain in and to enjoy. The garden layout or design was rigid, symetrical and formal with knots, hedges and colorful flowers. There were tennis courts, bowling greens and imitation animals.

In the 17th Century, design was influenced by the Renaissance. Many of the garden designers of this period were French, i.e.: the Huguenot Brothers and Isaac de Caus. The concept was that the house and garden should compliment each other. Most of the grand gardens of the pre-Civil War period were enclosed by walls and there was little connection with the surrounding landscape.

An increasing interest in the horticultural side of gardening developed during this time. This was demonstrated by the creation of the Oxford Botanical Garden in 1621 and the success of plant collectors such as John Tradescant and his son John who traveled not only to the continent but to the New World.

The Jacobeans and the Stuarts brought gardening to a fine art. One's garden became a reflection of one's status. Fountains and water features were used and topiaries became popular once again.

During the Restoration, in the later half of the 17th Century, the aristocracy brought back ideas from their travels in Europe and the French style was at its height. Smaller landowners began to take an interest in gardening. There was an increasing importance placed in the relationship between garden and surrounding countryside even during this period. This was to lay some of the foundation for the "landscape movement".

It was obvious that the New World had a wealth of horticultural treasures. The most extensive collection of North American trees and shrubs in England was aquired by Henry Compton for his garden at Fulham Palace. Compton, an influential figure in the plant trade, employed George London as gardener for several years starting in 1681.

The Dutch influence was also very popular. Their designs were geometric in their formality but smaller in scale than the French. The Dutch had also established themselves as plantsmen without equal and they displayed a true enjoyment in flower gardening.

Even with all these influences from Europe and America, England retained a clear measure of independence. Although much of what was created during this period was dramatically changed or even destroyed during the "Landscape Movement", the groundwork for England's future influence in the gardening field was established.

A few of the gardeners of the period were Charles Bridgeman, William Kent, George London and Henry Wise and Sir John Vanbrugh.

"LANDSCAPE MOVEMENT"- THE NATURAL LOOK

The Landscape Movement began in the early 18th Century and coincided with the Georgian period of architecture. It was a reaction to the formality and contrivances of the 17th century (topiaries, knot gardens, parterres) and a social reaction to the monarchy in favor of the landed gentry.

A respect for nature, "an essential factor of human life", became part of the philosophy of the time. It was felt that gardens should take their inspiration from nature. The garden became part of the countryside and the countryside came into the garden. Geometrical symmetry was replaced by asymmetry and serpentine curves.

Craftsmanship was also a part of the movement; wrought iron work was transformed into decorative gates and arbors and there were finely worked lead statues and urns.

The second half of the 18th Century was clearly dominated by Lancelot "Capability" Brown who carried the movement to an extreme. He created hundreds of acres of landscape parks. Hundreds of tons of dirt were moved to create a "natural" look, rivers were diverted or dammed and hills were built or removed. Hedges, parterres and flowers were removed, walls and fences were replaced by ha-has and architectural monuments became an integral part of the landscape.

Although horticulture took a backseat during this period, there was a continuing exchange of plant materials and ideas between England and the United States. The first varieties of rhododendrons and several ornamental trees and shrubs were imported from North America.

In the later part of the 18th Century, the "picturesque" movement developed. The preference was for a landscape of the natural scenery of mountains, streams and woodlands. This was again a reaction, but this time to Brown and his artificial landscapes.

Near the turn of the century Humphry Repton, who had initially followed in Brown's footsteps, was responsible for a transitional period when ornamental flower gardens and terraces were reintroduced into the "landscape".

A few of the gardeners of the period from England and the United States were Lancelot "Capability" Brown, Thomas Jefferson, Humphry Repton, George Washington.

VICTORIAN PERIOD

This was the real beginning of the English passion for gardening. The formal garden of the 17th century was reinstated. Huge and elaborate gardens were designed to compliment the flamboyant mansions of the period. Small cottage gardens became popular with the more prosperous middle class and even the working class had their window boxes.

The industrial revolution played a part in the new garden design. Coal furnaces heated greenhouses and the brick walls of kitchen gardens. Steam engines provided the power for garden fountains. The removal of the glass tax in 1845 opened the door to the building of conservatories and greenhouses. In addition, the wealth accumulated from industrial and commercial enterprises provided the money to create the great houses and gardens of this period.

The plant trade continued to grow. David Douglas introduced conifers from the United States, rhododendrons were introduced from the Himalayas and the fashionable scented-leafed geraniums were imported from South Africa.

This was the start of new gardening magazines and books, new kinds of garden tools and the first lawn mower which was invented in 1830.

Lawn was an essential element (made easier by the mower), roses were an important part of all the big estates and rock gardens were all the rage.

Americans greatly admired the public parks and gardens of the Victorian Period. F.L. Olmsted, an American landscape architect, visited England in 1850. His designs for parks such as Central Park in New York were greatly influenced by what he saw during his visit.

The Victorian influence remains in England today through the public parks and the colorful window boxes, hanging baskets and pots of geraniums, lobelia and aubretia seen throughout the country.

A few of the gardeners of the period were Humphry Repton, James Bateman, Robert Holford, Frederick Law Olmsted.

ARTS & CRAFTS MOVEMENT

In the last part of the 19th century in England, the Arts & Crafts Movement developed as a reaction to the ostentations of the Victorian period. It was a desire to emphasize craftsmanship, the qualities of the rural life and a more natural style.

At the center of the movement was designer William Morris who formed William Morris & Co. in 1861 with the goal of revitalizing the arts through craftsmanship. Morris, who was very fond of the Cotswolds, encouraged his friends to move there and a large number of craftsmen did move to Chipping Camden at the turn of the century

Munstead Wood in Surrey, designed by Edwin Lutyens for Gertrude Jekyll, is a good example of the movement. It incorporated Bargate stone walls, hand made tiles and mullion windows. Another example is Snowshill which was designed by Charles Wade, an architect of this period.

EARLY 20th CENTURY

The garden once again became social, a place for activity. It was no longer a place to merely be looked upon from the house but was something to be lived in, a continuation of the house with outdoor rooms.

The reaction to the Victorian garden took many forms. One was informal, a return to the natural look (the A & C Movement); another was formal in the overall look of the architecture and the garden. The third form provided a balance between architecture and horticulture, had an attention to details and could be adapted to any scale.

The biggest advocate for informality and more natural planting was William Robinson. Although a gardener in his own right, he was primarily a writer who had much influence on the designs of the day and on the future work of people like Gertrude Jekyll.

The model for the more formal gardens was the Italian Renaissance. Harold Peto and the water garden he designed at Buscot Park and Achille Duchene's water terrace at Blenheim Palace are good examples of this style.

The most lasting garden style was established by Gertrude Jekyll & Edwin Lutyens. Their gardens did not require expansive acreage and settings to achieve the desired affect and they demonstrated that the garden could have several looks throughout the year. They focused on regional architecture, local materials and placed a strong emphasis on plantsmanship. Future generations of designers and gardeners in England and America have followed their example and guidelines.

A few of the gardeners of the period were Gertrude Jekyll, Edwin Lutyens, Lawrence Johnston, Harold Peto, William Robinson, Achille Duchene.

MID 20th CENTURY

In the post World War I period, people did more of the gardening themselves. They looked for designs that were more understated and displayed planting rather than architectural monuments.

In the United States, Frank Lloyd Wright developed the "Prairie School" of architecture. During that same time Jans Jensen's garden designs became known as the "prairie style". An important part of his designs was his use of trees and plants that were native to a particular area.

In England a desire for informality was expressed in the creation of natural woodland gardens. Native trees, flowering and ornamental trees and shrubs and spring bulbs extended a garden's life throughout most of the year. The garden at the Rothschield estate, Exbury, was created during this period. Begun in 1919, it is over 200 acres of woodlands with a remarkable collection of rhododendrons and azaleas.

For most people, however, the typical 20th Century garden did not require hundreds of acres or famous designers. The style was "compartments", outdoor rooms with walls or hedges created out of hollies, yews or hornbeams as Lawrence Johnston did at Hidcote. The look was colorful borders with roses and perennials.

A few of the gardeners of the period were Lawrence Johnston, "Vita" Sackville-West, Thomas Church, Jans Jensen.

LATE 20th CENTURY

These are the days of the gifted "amateur" gardeners such as Penelope Hobhouse (one of my favorites), Christopher Lloyd and Rosemary Verey who, through their own gardens and their books and lectures, have reached a wider audience than many "professionals".

Garden styles have been borrowed from the past and mixed together with great freedom to create individual design and charm.

A few of the gardeners of the period are Penelope Hobhouse, Geoffrey Jellicoe, Christopher Lloyd, Rosemary Verey.

• GLOSSARY OF TERMS •

Allee- a formal hedged walk or road within the "wilderness". Be sure to see the hornbeam allee at Hidcote Manor.

Avenue- formed by successive pairs of trees or other identical shapes (pots or statues) flanking a drive, walk or pathway; gives a linear perspective and an impression of distance. See the many avenues radiating from the house at Buscot Park

Bog Garden- a marshy area with plants that love wet feet and need permanently saturated soil and almost no drainage. The garden at Upton House is one of the best I've ever seen.

Cottage Garden- a grand and colorful mixture of hollyhocks, sunflowers, pansies and roses, fruits, vegetables and lots of herbs. The garden beds, dating back to the 14th Century, overflow paths leading to the front of small country homes and are often duplicated as herbaceous borders in large estates and in suburban homes. Many of Gertrude Jekyll's ideas for borders were influenced by the cottage themes.

Elysium Fields- in Greek mythology, a place assigned to virtuous people after death; a place of ideal bliss; paradise. See the elysium fields at Farnborough Hall.

Espalier- a tree or row of trees (usually fruit) trained to grow flat on a latticework or trellis; see the kitchen garden at Painswick Rococo Garden and the old varieties at Westbury Court Garden.

Grotto- a hidden underground passage, an ornamental cave; usually containing a water feature. Remember to look for the grotto at Rousham.

Ha-Ha- a nearly invisible sunken barrier shaped like a ditch or dry moat, used instead of a raised barrier, wall or hedge to keep cattle out of the garden. It gives the illusion the garden and the surrounding countryside are one; see if you can spot the one at Hanbury Hall.

Herbaceous Border- beds of hardy perennials, many grown for cut flowers, originally planted to bloom for a short time in the summer but the new "mixed" border blooms from early spring until late fall; roses and peonies are often included. You will find these in every garden, after all it wouldn't be England without it, but some of the best are at Pusey, Miserden Park Gardens and Packwood House.

Knots- a pattern of intersecting bands of different herbs or low hedged planting beds; there are many examples in these tours, Sudeley Castle should not be missed.

Maze- a layout in which hedges are used to mark out a confusing pattern; the best known maze in England, planted in 1690, is in Hampton Court. A simple, yet well designed maze can be found at Blenheim Palace.

Obelisks- a tall, slender four sided pillar, gradually tapering as it rises, having the top in the form of a pyramid. One of these unusual monuments is featured at Farnborough Hall.

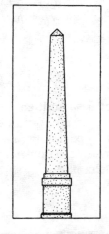

Orangery- orange trees were prized by English gardeners above almost any fruit and the orangery (or conservatory or greenhouse) was built to protect them and other tender plants from the winter cold. You must see Sezincote.

Parterre- the ornamental garden close to the palace or house, composed of low patterns in boxwood, grass or flowers; it was invented in the 16th century for the Queen of France. There are parterres in many gardens but the simple flower beds at Westbury Court are very special.

Pergola- a series of constructed arches that create a pathway and can be decorative or covered with climbing and twining plants. The laburnum walk at Barnsley House is a wonderful example for all seasons.

Pleaching- technique used for training and shaping trees into architectural forms they would not naturally take, done by bending and intertwining branches. See the wonderful pleached allee at Hidcote Manor.

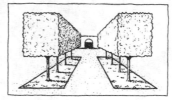

Potager- the vegetable or kitchen garden. There are certainly many examples, the one at Upton House is quite dramatic.

Topiary- clipped evergreens, some in elaborate forms, some in simple cones or pyramids. They came into their own in the 17th Century and were the first to go in the landscape movement. The Yew Garden at Packwood House is a good example of a simple cone shaped clipping; the White Garden at Hidcote Manor has several great little hens, doves and peacocks perched on hedges.

• GARDEN PARTICULARS •

	GARDEN NAME	CITY	PHONE NUMBER	NATIONAL TRUST	MONTHS OPEN	DAYS OPEN	HOURS OPEN	FEE/ AMOUNT	FOOD SERVICE	PICNIC AREA	REST ROOM	GIFT SHOP
1	Baddesley Clinton	Knowle	(01564) 783294	Yes	Mar-Sep Oct	Wed-Sun Wed-Sun	2:00-6:00 2:00-5:00	£4.50 chd £2.25	Yes	No	Yes	Yes
2	Barnsley House	Cirencester	(01285) 740281	No	All	Mon-Fri	10:00-6:00	£2.50,chd free	No	Yes	Yes	No
3	Batsford Park Arboretum	Moreton-in-Marsh	(01608) 650722	No	Mar-Nov	Daily	10:00-5:00	£2.00 chd £1.50	Yes	Yes	Yes	Yes
4	Berkeley Castle	Berkeley	(0453)810332	No	Apr May,Jun,Sept Jul & Aug May-Oct	Tues-Sun Tues-Sat Mon-Sat Sun	2:00-5:00 11:00-5:00 11:00-5:00 2:00-4:30	£4.50 chd £2.25	Yes	Yes	Yes	Yes
5	Blenheim Palace	Woodstock	(01993) 811091	No	Mid Mar to End Oct	Daily	10:30-5:30	Yes	Yes	Yes	Yes	Yes
6	Bourton House Garden	Bourton-on-the-Hill	(01386) 700121	No	May 23-Sep-27	Thurs,Fri	12:00-5:00	£2.50,chd free	Tea	No	Yes	No
7	Brook Cottage	Alkerton	(01295) 670303 or 670590	No	Apr thru Oct	Mon-Fri wknd by apt	9:00-6:00	£2.00,chd free	No	No	Yes	No
8	Broughton Castle	Banbury	(01295) 262624 (01869) 337126	No	Mid May-Mid Sep Jul & Aug	Wed & Sun Wed,Thu,Sun,Bk Hol	2:00-5:00 2:00-5:00	£3.50 chd £2.00	Tea	Yes	Yes	Yes
9	Buscot Park	Faringdon	(01367) 242094	Yes	Apr-Sep	Wed-Fri	2:00-6:00	£4.00	Yes	Yes	Yes	No
10	Charlecote Park	Warwick	(01789) 470277	Yes	Apr - Oct	Fri-Tues 2nd&4th Sat & Sun	11:00-6:00	£4.40 chd £2.20	Tea	Yes	Yes	Yes
11	Farnborough Hall	Banbury	(01295) 690202	Yes	Apr-Sep	Wed &Sat	2:00-6:00	£2.70	No	No	Yes	No
12	Hanbury Hall	Droitwich	(01527) 821214	Yes	Apr-Oct	Sun-Wed	2:00-6:00	£2.50 chd £1.00	Tea	No	Yes	Yes
13	Hidcote Manor Garden	Chipping Camden	(01386) 438333	Yes	Apr30 thru Sept Jun&Jul Oct	Daily ex Tu & Fr Tues Daily ex Tu & Fr	11:00-7:00 11:00-7:00 11:00-6:00	£5.20 chd £2.60	Yes	No	Yes	Yes
14	How Caple Court	How Caple	(01989) 740626	No	All Apr thr Oct	Mon-Sat Daily	9:30-5:00 10:00-5:00	£2.50 chd £1.25	Tea	No	Yes	Yes
15	Hunts Court	North Nibley	(01453) 547440	No	All ex Aug	Tues-Sat	9:00-5:00	£1.50	No	No	Yes	Nursery
16	Kiftsgate Court	Chipping Camden	(01386) 438777	No	Apr,May,Aug,Sep Jun,Jul	Wd,Th,Su Wd,Th,Sat,Su	2:00-6:00 12:00-6:00	£3.00 chd £1.00	Tea	No	Yes	No
17	Mallory Court Hotel	Leamington Spa	(01926) 330214	No	All	All	All	Hotel	4* Restaurant	No	Yes	No
18	Mill Garden	Warwick	(01926) 492877	No	All	Daily	9:00-dusk	£1.00,chd free	No	No	Yes	No
19	Miserden Park	Miserden	(01285) 821303	No	Apr 1-Sep 26	Tue,Wed & Thur	9:30-4:30	£2.50,chd free	Tea	No	Yes	Nursery
20	Oxford University Botanic Garden	Oxford	(01865) 276920	No	All	Daily	9:00-5:00	£1.00,chd free	No	No	No	No

THE MONTHS, DAYS AND TIMES OF OPERATION WERE CONFIRMED PRIOR TO PUBLICATION OF THIS BOOK. THE AUTHOR IS NOT RESPONSIBLE IF CHANGES ARE MADE TO THESE SCHEDULES. IT IS ADVISABLE TO CONFIRM THE SCHEDULE PRIOR TO SETTING OUT ON YOUR DAY'S TOUR.

• GARDEN PARTICULARS •

	GARDEN NAME	CITY	PHONE NUMBER	NATIONAL TRUST	MONTHS OPEN	DAYS OPEN	HOURS OPEN	FEE/ AMOUNT	FOOD SERVICE	PICNIC AREA	REST ROOM	GIFT SHOP
21	Packwood House	Lapworth	(01564) 782024	Yes	Apr to end Sept Oct	Wed-Sun Wed-Sun	2:00-6:00 12:30-4:30	£3.30 chd £1.90	No	Yes	Yes	Yes
22	Painswick Rococo Garden	Painswick	(01452) 813204	No	Jan 10-Nov 30 Jul-Aug	Wed-Sun,Bk Hol Daily	11:00-5:00 11:00-5:00	£2.75 chd £1.50	Yes	No	Yes	Yes
23	The Priory	Kemerton	(01386) 725258	No	May31-Sep28	Fri	11:00-5:00	£2.00,chd free	No	No	No	No
24	Pusey	Faringdon		No	Apr to Oct	Daily exc Mon & Fri Bk Hol wknds Sat-Mon	2:00-6:00	Yas	No	No	No	No
25	Rousham Park	Steeple Aston	(0869)347110	No	All	Daily	10:00-4:30	£2.50 no chd under 15	No	Yes	Yes	No
26	Sezincote	Moreton-in-Marsh		No	May-Jul&Sept	Thur, Fr, Bk Hol	2:00-6:00	£3.00 chd £1.00	No	No	Yes	No
27	Snowshill Manor	Broadway	(01386) 852410	Yes	Apr & Oct May to Sept	Daily ex Tue Daily exTue	1:00 -5:00 1:00-6:00	£5.20 chd £2.60	Yes	No	Yes	Yes
28	Spetchley Park	Spetchley	(01905)345213 (01905)345224	No	Apr thr Sept	Tues-Fri Sun	11:00-5:00 2:00-5:30	£2.50 chc £1.20	Yes	Yes	Yes	Yes
29	Stowe Landscape Gardens	Buckingham	(01280) 822850	Yes	Apr15-Jul5 Jul7-Sep8	Mon,Wed,Fri,Sun Daily	10:00-5:00 10:00-5:00	£4.00	Yes	Yes	Yes	Yes
30	Sudeley Castle	Winchcombe	(01242) 603197 or 602308	No	Apr thru Oct Mar	Daily Daily	11:00-5:00 10:30-4:30	£4.00 chd £1.80	Yes	Yes	Yes	Yes
31	Upton House	Banbury	(01295) 670266	Yes	Apr -Oct	Sat-Wed	2:00-6:00	£4.60 chd £2.40	Tea	No	Yes	Yes
32	Waddesdon Manor	Waddesdon	(01296) 651282	Yes	Mar-Dec	Wed-Sun	11:00-5:00	£3.00 chd £1.50	Yes	Yes	Yes	Yes
33	Warwick Castle	Warwick	(01926) 406600	No	All	All	10:00-6:00	£3.00 chd £5.00	Yes	Yes	Yes	Yes
34	Waterperry Hort. Center	Wheatley	(01844) 339226 or 339254	No	All	Daily	10:00-6:00	£2.30 chc £1.00	Tea	Yes	Yes	Garden Center
35	Westbury Garden Court	Westbury-on-Seven	(01452) 760461	Yes	Apr - Oct	Wed-Sun	11:00-6:30	£2.50 chd £1.25	No	Yes	No	No
36	Westonbirt Arboretum	Tetbury	(01666) 880220	No	All	Daily	10:00-8:00	£2.80 chd £1.00	Yes	Yes	Yes	Yes
37	Whichford Pottery	Whichford	01608 684416		All	Mon-Fri Sat	9:00-5:30 10:00-4:00	Pottery				

THE MONTHS, DAYS AND TIMES OF OPERATION WERE CONFIRMED PRIOR TO PUBLICATION OF THIS BOOK. THE AUTHOR IS NOT RESPONSIBLE IF CHANGES ARE MADE TO THESE SCHEDULES.
IT IS ADVISABLE TO CONFIRM THE SCHEDULE PRIOR TO SETTING OUT ON YOUR DAYS TOUR.

• LIST OF PUBLICATIONS •

Garden Books

"Yellow Book", Gardens of England and Wales, for a copy send $18.00 to: The National Gardens Scheme, Hatchlands Park, East Clandon, Guildford, Surrey, GU4 7RT

Garden Style by Penelope Hobhouse; Little, Brown & Company, 1988

A Book of Gardening- The National Trust by Penelope Hobhouse; Little, Brown & Company, 1986

Flower Gardens by Penelope Hobhouse, Little, Brown & Co., 1991

The Ordnance Survey Guide to Gardens in England; W.W. Norton & Company, 1986

The Country House Garden by Gervase Jackson-Stops; Pavilion Books Limited, 1987

The Garden Makers by George Plumptre; Random House, 1993

One Hundred English Gardens by Patrick Taylor; Rizzoli International Publications, Inc, 1996

The National Trust Gardens Handbook, for a copy contact: The National Trust, 36 Queen Anne's Gate, London SW1H 9AS or phone 0171 222 9251

Gardens of the National Trust by Graham Thomas, The National Trust/Weidenfeld & Nicolson, London, 1979

Gardens of England, Scotland & Wales By Hazel Evens, George Philip Limited, 1991

The History of Gardens by Christopher Thacker, University of California Press, 1979

The Art of Planting by Rosemary Verey, Little, Brown & Co., 1990

• LIST OF PUBLICATIONS •

Hotels and B & B's

Bed and Breakfast for Garden Lovers, for a copy send a self addressed envelope with 3 international reply-paid coupons to: BBGL, Handywater Farm, Sibford Gower, Banbury, Oxfordshire OX15 5AE

Cotswold Retreats, for a copy call: Paula at 01608 737222 or Sue at 01608 684310 or fax 01608 684310

The National Trust Bed and Breakfast, for a copy contact: The National Trust, 36 Queen Anne's Gate, London SW1H 9AS or phone 0171 222 9251

England, Charming Bed & Breakfasts; Karen Brown; Travel Press, 1996 or phone (415) 342-9117

England, Wales & Scotland, Charming Hotels & Itineraries; Karen Brown; Travel Press, 1996 or phone (415) 342-9117

Index

• ORDER FORM •

For additional copies of this book:

- Fax Orders: (510) 934-8002 (send this form)
- On-Line orders: Bonnie Randall-- rpd@lanminds.com
- Postal Orders: Windsor Hill Publishing,
  119 Poppy Court, Walnut Creek, Ca. 94596, U.S.A.
- Telephone orders: (510) 934 7761

Please send _____ additional copies of *Garden Tours of England -The Cotswolds* at a cost of $14.95 per copy.

Sales tax for those books shipped in California is 8.25%.

Shipping: Book rate is $2.00 for the first book and 75 cents for each additional book (shipping may take 3 to 4 weeks). Air Mail is $3.50 per book.

Please Print:

Name:_____

Address:_____

City:_____ State_____ Zip:_____

Telephone:_____

		Total
Tour Books	_____ x $14.95	
Tax	8.25% in Calif.	
Shipping		
Total		

Payment:
☐ Check

◻ Credit Card: ◻ VISA, ◻ MasterCard

Card number:_____ Exp Date:_____

Name on card:_____

Signature:_____

• ORDER FORM •

For additional copies of this book:

- Fax Orders: (510) 934-8002 (send this form)
- On-Line orders: Bonnie Randall-- rpd@lanminds.com
- Postal Orders: Windsor Hill Publishing,
  119 Poppy Court, Walnut Creek, Ca. 94596, U.S.A.
- Telephone orders: (510) 934-7761

Please send _____ additional copies of *Garden Tours of England -The Cotswolds* at a cost of $14.95 per copy.

Sales tax for those books shipped in California is 8.25%.

Shipping: Book rate is $2.00 for the first book and 75 cents for each additional book (shipping may take 3 to 4 weeks). Air Mail is $3.50 per book.

Please Print:

Name:_____

Address:_____

City:_____State_____Zip:_____

Telephone:_____

		Total
Tour Books	_____x $14.95	
Tax	8.25% in Calif.	
Shipping		
Total		

Payment:
▫ Check

▫ Credit Card: ▫ VISA, ▫ MasterCard

Card number:_____Exp Date:_____

Name on card:_____

Signature:_____